Guinness
Book of
Women's
Sports Records

Guinness
Book of
Women's
Sports Records

Norris McWhirter · Steve Morgenstern
Roz Morgenstern · Stan Greenberg

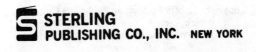
STERLING
PUBLISHING CO., INC.   NEW YORK

GUINNESS FAMILY OF BOOKS

Air Facts and Feats
Animal Facts and Feats
Boating Facts and Feats
Car Facts and Feats
Towers, Bridges and Other
Structures

Guinness Book of Essential
Facts
Guinness Sports Record
Book
Guinness Book of Women's
Sports Records
Guinness Book of Amazing
Achievements

Guinness Book of Astounding
Feats and Events
Guinness Book of Daring
Deeds & Fascinating Facts
Guinness Book of
Exceptional Experiences
Guinness Book of
Extraordinary Exploits
Guinness Book of
Phenomenal Happenings
Guinness Book of Startling
Acts and Facts
Guinness Book of Surprising
Accomplishments
Guinness Book of Young
Recordbreakers

The editors and publishers wish to thank the following people and organizations for pictures which they supplied:

Associated Newspapers Ltd.; Associated Press; Franklin Berger; William Berry; The Bodley Head; Central Press Photos Ltd.; Gerry Cranham; Tony Duffy; Mary Evans, Harrap; Hart Picture Archives; Keystone Press Agency Ltd.; E. D. Lacey; Ladies Professional Golf Association; *Manchester Guardian;* Don Morley; *News Chronicle;* Novosti Press Agency, Moscow; Photo-Reportage Ltd.; Popperfoto; Press Association Photos; Race Course Technical Services; Radio Times Hulton Picture Library; Leon S. Serchuk; George A. Smallsreid, U.S. Trotting Association; Sonja Henie Og Niels Onstads Stiftelser; Sport and General Press Agency Ltd.; United Press International; United States Lawn Tennis Association; Virginia Slims; Wide World Photos; Women's International Bowling Congress.

Our thanks also to the Amateur Athletic Union of the United States, who supplied the U.S. swimming and track and field records included in this volume.

Contents

Introduction

In this Guinness record book you will find the finest women's athletic performances in over three dozen sports, including world, national and Olympic competition. Here are the popular superstars alongside the lesser known champions. The golfers and tennis players are represented, and so are the archers, bull fighters, swimmers and water skiers. You will meet the pioneers who opened the door, and the record holders of today who are building a rich and lasting tradition of athletic achievement which serves as an inspiration to rising young athletes and a source of pride for all women.

With the tremendous growth and popularity of women's sports throughout the world, interest in women participating on both the amateur and professional levels has moved in dramatic directions. Games that were formerly simply to pass the time have now developed into sports in which women find self-satisfaction in pushing their bodies and skills to the limit. The woman who makes a serious commitment to training for a sport is increasingly accepted and admired by society. Millions of women of all ages now enjoy the sense of accomplishment which comes from competing with other women, with men, and with themselves.

With the publicity that is now given to women's spectator sports, professionals have soared to greater heights in earnings than anyone expected 10 years ago. Media coverage has sparked widespread interest throughout the population, so that both men and women regularly view women's sports on television today. After years of determined battle, women athletes are finally achieving equality with men in the playing conditions and prizes for their competitions. Today's woman professional athlete is out to win not just for the joy of winning, but for fame and money as well.

Here then are the facts about the amateurs and the professionals, the historical greats and the current stars, the sweat and pain and the dollars and cents of women's sports.

Sports, Games and Pastimes

Earliest

The origins of sport stem from the time when self-preservation ceased to be the all-consuming human preoccupation. Archery was a hunting skill in Mesolithic times (by *c.*8000 B.C.), but did not become an organized sport until about 300 A.D., among the Genoese. The earliest dated evidence for sport is *c.*2450 B.C. for fowling with throwing sticks and hunting. Ball games by girls, depicted on Middle Kingdom murals at Beni Hasan, Egypt, have been dated to *c.*2050 B.C. Despite this early evidence of women's participation in sporting activities, it is only in fairly recent times that women have taken part—indeed, in most cultures, been allowed to take part—in a wide range of sports.

Women were barred from the ancient Olympic Games to the extent that they were not even allowed to watch, but this does not indicate a total lack of athletic activity by women at the time. The legend of Atalanta, who was abandoned in the wild and brought up by a she-bear, indicates this. She became a huntress renowned for her running ability. If a suitor wanted her in marriage he had to beat her in a foot race—if he lost he was killed. Many died, until Milanion, on the advice of Aphrodite, dropped golden apples to distract Atalanta, and thus beat her.

On a somewhat more historical note, Spartan women were taught running, wrestling and throwing the discus and javelin from an early age. This led to the establishment of the Heraean Games, which offered a limited number of events to these early Greek athletes. To set the record straight, it is not exactly true to say that women were completely barred from Olympic competition, since they could actually "win" an Olympic title as owner of a winning chariot. The first such "proxy" winner was Cynisca of Sparta in 396 B.C.

Women first competed in the modern Olympic Games in 1900, in tennis and golf. The first gold medallists were Charlotte Cooper of Great Britain, who won the ladies' singles tennis title, and Margaret Abbott of the U.S. who won the nine-hole women's golf competition. It was not until 1924 that women had a reasonably full program of Olympic sports.

Though the ancient Greek and Roman women wore quite skimpy attire in their Games, in recent historical times the demands of etiquette, which frowned on the exposure of even an ankle, greatly inhibited those pioneers who attempted games and sports. It was not until 1919 that Elaine Burton, later a British Member of Parliament, became the first sports-woman to run in shorts, while a similar fashion in tennis was not introduced in America until the 1930's by Helen Hull Jacobs.

Youngest World Record Breaker

The youngest age at which any person has broken a world record is 12 years 298 days in the case of Gertrude Ederle (born October 23, 1906) of the United States, who broke the women's 880-yard freestyle swimming world record with 13 minutes 19.0 seconds at Indianapolis, Indiana on August 17, 1919.

Youngest International

The youngest age at which any person has won international honors is 8 years old in the case of Joy Foster, the Jamaican singles and mixed-doubles table tennis champion in 1958.

Youngest Olympic Winner

The youngest person to win an individual Olympic gold medal was Marjorie Gestring of the U.S., who took the spring-board diving title at the age of 13 years 9 months at the Olympic Games in Berlin in 1936.

Janet Lynn smiles after signing her record $1,500,000 contract with Shipstad and Johnson Ice Follies.

Greatest Earnings

The greatest fortune amassed by a woman in sport is an estimated $47,500,000 by Sonja Henie (1912–69) of Norway, the triple Olympic figure-skating champion, who followed her amateur success by becoming a professional ice-skating promoter and starring in her own ice shows and motion pictures.

The highest-paid woman athlete in the world is ice skater Janet Lynn (born April 6, 1953) (*née* Nowicki) of the U.S., who signed a $1,500,000 three-year contract in 1974. In the same year she earned more than $750,000.

Most Versatile Athletes

Charlotte (Lottie) Dod (1870–1960) won the Wimbledon singles title five times between 1887–93, the British Ladies Golf Championship in 1904, an Olympic silver medal for archery in 1908, and represented England at hockey in 1899.

As both amateur and professional, Mildred (Babe) Didrikson Zaharias (born Port Arthur, Texas, June 26, 1914; died September 27, 1956) competed at the championship level in an unparalleled array of sports. She was an All-American basketball player for three consecutive years, 1930–32, playing for the

Employers Casualty Company team. At the 1932 Olympic Games in Los Angeles she won two gold medals, in the javelin throw and the 80-meter hurdles, setting world records in each, and a silver medal in the high jump.

She turned professional after the Games and trained as a boxer briefly, then switched to golf, where she had many of her greatest triumphs, including virtually every major title at least once, between 1940 and 1950. She also excelled at billiards, lacrosse, swimming, diving and place-kicking. She holds the women's world record for longest throw of a baseball, with a 296-foot throw at Jersey City, New Jersey, on July 25, 1931.

No other athlete, male or female, has displayed sports versatility on the championship level to compare with Babe Didrikson. Among her many honors, she was named Greatest Female Athlete of the Half Century by the Associated Press in 1949.

Comparative Speed Records

There is great controversy in the world of sport today regarding the possibility of a woman rivalling the men's world records in track and field or swimming events. Research differs regarding the nature of a woman's ability to train her body for strength comparable to a man's, despite the unchangeable physical differences between the sexes. The issue is further clouded by the emotional and sociological factors which combine to limit the opportunities and motivation for women's athletic achievement throughout the world.

On the following pages are comparative charts of women's and men's progressive achievements in track and in swimming which are of interest in themselves, and provide some raw data for putting the sometimes excessive statements made on both sides of the argument in some sort of perspective.

TRACK

100 Meters

Women
sec.

Men
sec.

11.0 Harald Andersson-Arbin (Sweden), 1890

10.8 Luther Cary (U.S.), 1891

10.6 Knut Lindberg (Sweden), 1906

10.5 Richard Rau (Germany), 1911

12.8 Marie Kiessling (Germany), 1921

10.4 Charlie Paddock (U.S.), 1921

12.6 Gundel Wittmann (Germany), 1926

12.4 Gundel Wittmann (Germany), 1926

12.4 Eileen Edwards (G.B.), 1927

12.2 Elizabeth Robinson (U.S.), 1927

12.1 Hilde Gladitsch (Germany), 1927

The 100 meter record set by Jim Hines (right) has remained, while runners like Renate Stecher (left) continue to improve the women's mark.

12.0 Elizabeth Robinson (U.S.), 1928

                    10.3 Percy Williams (Canada), 1930

11.9 Tollien Schuurman (Neth.), 1932
11.8 Stella Walasiewicz (Poland), 1933
11.7 Stella Walasiewicz (Poland), 1934
11.6 Helen Stephens (U.S.), 1935
11.5 Helen Stephens (U.S.), 1936   10.2 Jesse Owens (U.S.), 1936

                    10.1 Lloyd La Beach (Panama), 1950

11.4 Marjorie Jackson (Australia), 1952
11.3 Shirley De La Hunty (Australia), 1955

                    10.1 Armin Hary (W. Germany), 1960

11.2 Wilma Rudolph (U.S.), 1961
11.1 Irena Kirszenstein (Poland), 1965
11.0 Wyomia Tyus (U.S.), 1968   9.9 Jim Hines (U.S.), 1968
10.9 Renate Stecher (E. Germany), 1973
10.8 Renate Stecher (E. Germany), 1973

400 Meters

Figures indicated with an asterisk are converted from 440 yards time.

Women	Men
sec.	sec.
	48.9* Lon Myers (U.S.), 1879
	48.5* Lon Myers (U.S.), 1881
	48.2* Lenox Tindall (G.B.), 1889
	47.5* Maxie Long (U.S.), 1900
	47.1* Ted Meredith (U.S.), 1916
62.1* Mary Lines (G.B.), 1923	
60.5* Vera Palmer (G.B.), 1923	
	47.0 Emerson Spencer (U.S.), 1928
60.3* Marian King (G.B.), 1929	
58.9* Marian King (G.B.), 1929	
58.5* Nellie Halstead (G.B.), 1931	
56.5* Nellie Halstead (G.B.), 1932	46.1* Ben Eastman (U.S.), 1932
	46.0 Rudolf Harbig (Germany), 1939
	45.9 Herb McKenley (Jamaica), 1946
	45.7 Herb McKenley (Jamaica), 1948
56.0 Zoya Petrova (U.S.S.R.), 1951	
55.7 Ursula Donath (E. Germany), 1953	
55.5 Nina Otkalenko (U.S.S.R.), 1954	
55.0 Ursula Donath (E. Germany), 1954	
54.8 Zinaida Safronova (U.S.S.R.), 1955	45.4 Lou Jones (U.S.), 1955
54.4 Ursula Donath (E. Germany), 1955	
53.9 Maria Itkina (U.S.S.R.), 1955	45.2 Lou Jones (U.S.), 1956
53.6 Maria Itkina (U.S.S.R.), 1957	
53.4 Maria Itkina (U.S.S.R.), 1959	
53.0 Sin Kim Dan (N. Korea), 1960	44.9 Otis Davis (U.S.), 1960
51.9 Sin Kim Dan (N. Korea), 1962	

51.4 Sin Kim Dan (N. Korea),
      1963
51.2 Sin Kim Dan (N. Korea),
      1964

51.0 Marilyn Neufville
      (Jamaica), 1970
49.9 Irena Szewinska (Poland),
      1974
49.8 Christina Brehmer
      (E. Germany), 1976
49.3 Irena Szewinska (Poland),
      1976
49.2 Maritta Koch
      (E. Germany), 1978
49.0 Maritta Koch
      (E. Germany), 1978
48.9 Maritta Koch
      (E. Germany), 1978

44.6 Adolph Plummer (U.S.),
      1963

44.5 Tommie Smith (U.S.), 1967
44.4 Vince Matthews (U.S.),
      1968
44.0 Lee Evans (U.S.), 1968
43.8 Lee Evans (U.S.), 1968

1,500 Meters

Women

min. : sec.
(Rarely run prior to 1950's)

Men

min. : sec.
3:59.8 Harold Wilson (G.B.), 1908
3:59.2 Abel Kiviat (U.S.), 1912
3:55.8 Abel Kiviat (U.S.), 1912
3:54.7 John Zander (Sweden),
        1917
3:53.0 Paavo Nurmi (Finland),
        1923
3:52.6 Paavo Nurmi (Finland),
        1924
3:51.0 Otto Pelzer (Germany),
        1926
3:49.2 Jules Ladoumegue
        (France), 1930
3:49.0 Luigi Beccali (Italy), 1933
3:48.8 Bill Bonthron (U.S.), 1934
3:47.8 Jack Lovelock (New
        Zealand), 1936

3:47.6 Gunder Hägg (Sweden),
1941
3:45.8 Gunder Hägg (Sweden),
1942
3:45.0 Arne Andersson
(Sweden), 1943
3:43.0 Gunder Hägg (Sweden),
1944

4:37.8 Olga Ovsyannikova
(U.S.S.R.), 1946
4:37.0 Nina Otkalenko
(U.S.S.R.), 1952

3:42.8 Wes Santee (U.S.), 1954
3:41.8 John Landy (Australia),
1954
3:40.8 Sandor Iharos (Hungary),
1955
4:35.4 Phyllis Perkins (G.B.),
1956
3:40.6 Istvan Rozsavolgyi
(Hungary), 1956
4:30.0 Diane Leather (G.B.), 1957
3:40.2 Olavi Salsola (Finland),
1957
4:29.7 Diane Leather (G.B.), 1957
3:38.1 Stanislav Jungwirth
(Czech.), 1957
3:36.0 Herb Elliott (Australia),
1958
3:35.6 Herb Elliott (Australia),
1960

4:19.0 Marise Chamberlain
(New Zealand), 1962
4:17.3 Anne Smith (G.B.), 1967
3:33.1 Jim Ryun (U.S.), 1967
4:12.4 Paola Pigni (Italy), 1969
4:10.7 Jaroslava Jehlickova
(Czech.), 1969
4:09.6 Karin Burneleit
(E. Germany), 1971
4:06.9 Ludmila Bragina
(U.S.S.R.), 1972
4:06.5 Ludmila Bragina
(U.S.S.R.), 1972
4:05.1 Ludmila Bragina
(U.S.S.R.), 1972
4:01.4 Ludmila Bragina
(U.S.S.R.), 1972

3:32.2 Filbert Bayi (Tanzania),
1974

3:56.0 Tatyana Kazankina
(U.S.S.R.), 1976

SWIMMING

100 Meter Freestyle

Women	Men
sec.	*sec.*
	65.8 Zoltan Halmay (Hungary), 1905
95.0 Martha Gerstung (Germany), 1908	65.6 Charles Daniels (U.S.), 1908
86.6 C. Guttenstein (Belgium), 1910	62.8 Charles Daniels (U.S.), 1910
84.6 Daisy Curwen (G.B.), 1911	
80.6 Daisy Curwen (G.B.), 1912	62.4 Kurt Bretting (Germany), 1912
79.8 Fanny Durack (Australia), 1912	61.6 Duke Kahanamoku (U.S.), 1912
78.8 Fanny Durack (Australia), 1912	
76.2 Fanny Durack (Australia), 1915	
	61.4 Duke Kahanamoku (U.S.), 1918
73.6 Ethelda Bleibtrey (U.S.), 1920	60.4 Duke Kahanamoku (U.S.), 1920
	58.6 Johnny Weissmuller (U.S.), 1922
72.8 Gertrude Ederle (U.S.), 1923	
72.2 Mariechen Wehselau (U.S.), 1924	57.4 Johnny Weissmuller (U.S.), 1924
70.0 Ethel Lackie (U.S.), 1926	
69.8 Eleanora Garratti (U.S.), 1929	
69.4 Albina Osipowich (U.S.), 1929	
68.0 Helene Madison (U.S.), 1930	
66.6 Helene Madison (U.S.), 1931	
66.0 Willy den Ouden (Neth.), 1933	
65.4 Willy den Ouden (Neth.), 1934	56.8 Peter Fick (U.S.), 1934
64.8 Willy den Ouden (Neth.), 1934	
	56.6 Peter Fick (U.S.), 1935
64.6 Willy den Ouden (Neth.), 1936	56.4 Peter Fick (U.S.), 1936
	55.9 Alan Ford (U.S.), 1944
	55.8 Alex Jany (France), 1947

Dawn Fraser, who shares the record for total Olympic swimming medals won, held the women's record for the 100 meter freestyle event from 1956–1964.

55.4 Alan Ford (U.S.), 1948
54.8 Dick Cleveland (U.S.), 1954

64.5 Dawn Fraser (Australia), 1956
64.2 Cockie Gastelaars (Neth.), 1956
64.0 Cockie Gastelaars (Neth.), 1956
63.3 Dawn Fraser (Australia), 1956
63.2 Lorraine Crapp (Australia), 1956
62.4 Lorraine Crapp (Australia), 1956
62.0 Dawn Fraser (Australia), 1956

54.6 John Devitt (Australia), 1957

61.5 Dawn Fraser (Australia), 1958
61.4 Dawn Fraser (Australia), 1958
61.2 Dawn Fraser (Australia), 1958
60.2 Dawn Fraser (Australia), 1960

54.4 Steve Clark (U.S.), 1961
53.6 Manuel dos Santos (Brazil), 1961

60.0 Dawn Fraser (Australia), 1962

59.9 Dawn Fraser (Australia),
1962
59.5 Dawn Fraser (Australia),
1962
58.9 Dawn Fraser (Australia),
1964

52.9 Alain Gottvalles (France),
1964
52.6 Ken Walsh (U.S.), 1967
52.2 Mike Wenden (Australia),
1968
51.9 Mark Spitz (U.S.), 1970

58.5 Shane Gould (Australia),
1972

51.47 Mark Spitz (U.S.), 1972

51.22 Mark Spitz (U.S.), 1972

58.25 Kornelia Ender
(E. Germany), 1973
58.12 Kornelia Ender
(E. Germany), 1973
57.61 Kornelia Ender
(E. Germany), 1974
56.96 Kornelia Ender
(E. Germany), 1974
56.38 Kornelia Ender
(E. Germany), 1975
56.22 Kornelia Ender
(E. Germany), 1975

51.12 Jim Montgomery (U.S.),
1975
51.11 Andy Coan (U.S.), 1975

50.59 Jim Montgomery (U.S.),
1975

55.73 Kornelia Ender
(E. Germany), 1976
55.65 Kornelia Ender
(E. Germany), 1976
55.41 Barbara Krause
(E. Germany), 1978

49.99 Jim Montgomery (U.S.),
1976
49.44 Jonty Skinner (S. Africa),
1976

1,500 Meter Freestyle

Women

min.: sec.
21:45.7 Ragnhild Hveger
(Denmark), 1938
21:10.1 Ragnhild Hveger
(Denmark), 1940
20:57.0 Ragnhild Hveger
(Denmark), 1941

Men

min.: sec.
18:58.8 Tomikatsu Amano
(Japan), 1938

18:19.0 Hironashin Furuhashi
(Japan), 1949

20:45.6 Lenie de Nijs (Neth.),
1955
20:22.8 Jans Koster (Neth.), 1956

18:05.9 George Breen (U.S.), 1956
17:59.5 Murray Rose
(Australia), 1956
17:52.9 George Breen (U.S.), 1956

20:03.1 Jans Koster (Neth.), 1957

17:28.7 Jon Konrads (Australia),
1958

19:25.7 Ilsa Konrads (Australia),
1959
19:23.6 Jane Cederqvist
(Sweden), 1960

17:11.0 Jon Konrads (Australia),
1960

19:02.8 Margareta Rylander
(Sweden), 1961
18:44.0 Carolyn Howel (U.S.),
1962

17:05.5 Roy Saari (U.S.), 1963
18:30.5 Patty Caretto (U.S.),
1964

17:01.8 Murray Rose (Australia),
1964
16:58.7 Roy Saari (U.S.), 1964
18:23.7 Patty Caretto (U.S.),
1965

16:58.6 Steve Krause (U.S.), 1965
18:12.9 Patty Caretto (U.S.),
1966

16:41.6 Mike Burton (U.S.), 1966
18:11.1 Debbie Meyer (U.S.),
1967

16:34.1 Mike Burton (U.S.), 1967
17:50.2 Debbie Meyer (U.S.),
1967
17:31.2 Debbie Meyer (U.S.),
1968

16:28.1 Guillermo Echeverria
(Mex.), 1968

In 1968 and 1969 a series of records for the
1,500 meter freestyle were set by Debbie
Meyer (left) and Mike Burton (above).

17:19.9 Debbie Meyer (U.S.),
1969

16:08.5 Mike Burton (U.S.), 1968
16:04.5 Mike Burton (U.S.), 1969

15:57.1 John Kinsella (U.S.),
1970

17:19.2 Cathy Calhoun (U.S.),
1971
17:00.6 Shane Gould (Australia),
1971

15:52.91 Rick DeMont (U.S.),
1972
15:52.58 Mike Burton (U.S.),
1972

16:56.9 Shane Gould (Australia),
1973
15:37.8 Steve Holland
(Australia), 1973
16:54.14 Jo Harshbarger (U.S.),
1973
15:31.85 Steve Holland
(Australia), 1973
16:49.9 Jenny Turrall (Australia),
1973
16:48.2 Jenny Turrall (Australia),
1974
15:31.75 Tim Shaw (U.S.), 1974
16:43.4 Jenny Turrall (Australia),
1974
16:39.28 Jenny Turrall
(Australia), 1974
16:33.94 Jenny Turrall
(Australia), 1974

15:27.79 Steve Holland
(Australia), 1975
15:20.91 Tim Shaw (U.S.), 1975
15:10.59 Steve Holland
(Australia), 1976
15:06.66 Brian Goodell (U.S.),
1976
15:02.40 Brian Goodell (U.S.),
1976

16:24.60 Alice Browne (U.S.),
1977
16:14.93 Tracey Wickham
(Australia), 1978

100 Meter Butterfly

Became a separate event in 1952.

Women
sec.

76.6 Jutta Langenau
    (E. Germany), 1954
74.0 Shelley Mann (U.S.), 1954

73.8 Mary Kok (Neth.), 1955
73.7 Atie Voorbij (Neth.), 1955
73.2 Atie Voorbij (Neth.), 1955
73.1 Atie Voorbij (Neth.), 1955
71.9 Atie Voorbij (Neth.), 1956
71.8 Shelley Mann (U.S.), 1956
70.5 Atie Voorbij (Neth.), 1956

69.6 Nancy Ramey (U.S.), 1958

69.1 Nancy Ramey (U.S.), 1959

68.9 Jan Andrew (Australia), 1961
68.8 Mary Stewart (Canada),
    1961
68.2 Susan Doerr (U.S.), 1961
67.8 Susan Doerr (U.S.), 1962
67.3 Mary Stewart (Canada),
    1962
66.5 Kathy Ellis (U.S.), 1963
66.1 Ada Kok (Neth.), 1963
65.4 Sharon Stouder (U.S.), 1964
65.1 Ada Kok (Neth.), 1964
64.7 Sharon Stouder (U.S.), 1964
64.5 Ada Kok (Neth.), 1965

Men
sec.

64.3 Gyorgy Tumpek (Hungary),
    1953
63.7 Gyorgy Tumpek (Hungary),
    1954
62.3 Gyorgy Tumpek (Hungary),
    1954
62.1 Gyorgy Tumpek (Hungary),
    1954
62.0 Gyorgy Tumpek (Hungary),
    1954

61.5 Albert Wiggins (U.S.), 1955

61.3 Takashi Ishimoto (Japan),
    1957
61.2 Takashi Ishimoto (Japan),
    1957
61.0 Takashi Ishimoto (Japan),
    1958
60.1 Takashi Ishimoto (Japan),
    1958

59.0 Lance Larson (U.S.), 1960
58.7 Lance Larson (U.S.), 1960
58.6 Fred Schmidt (U.S.), 1961

58.4 Luis Nicolao (Argent.), 1962
57.0 Luis Nicolao (Argent.), 1962

56.3 Mark Spitz (U.S.), 1967

55.7 Mark Spitz (U.S.), 1967
55.6 Mark Spitz (U.S.), 1968

64.1 Alice Jones (U.S.), 1970

55.0 Mark Spitz (U.S.), 1971
63.9 Mayumi Aoki (Japan), 1972
54.72 Mark Spitz (U.S.), 1972
63.80 Andrea Gyarmati
54.56 Mark Spitz (U.S.), 1972
(Hungary), 1972
63.34 Mayumi Aoki (Japan), 1972
54.27 Mark Spitz (U.S.), 1972
63.05 Kornelia Ender
(E. Germany), 1973
62.31 Kornelia Ender
(E. Germany), 1973
62.09 Rosemarie Kother
(E. Germany), 1974
61.99 Rosemarie Kother
(E. Germany), 1974
61.88 Rosemarie Kother
(E. Germany), 1974
61.33 Kornelia Ender
(E. Germany), 1975
61.24 Kornelia Ender
(E. Germany), 1975
60.13 Kornelia Ender
(E. Germany), 1976
59.78 Christiane Knacke
54.18 Joe Bottom (U.S.), 1977
(E. Germany), 1977
59.46 Andrea Pollack
(E. Germany), 1978

The record set by Joe Bottom in 1977 for the 100 meter butterfly was over 5.5 seconds faster than Christiane Knacke's new record of the same year.

Archery

The discovery of stone arrowheads at Border Cave, Northern Natal, South Africa, indicates the invention of the bow and arrow came before 46,000 B.C. Archery as a sport developed at least as early as the 3rd century A.D.

The Amazons of ancient Greece were said to have been archers, and it is certain that the so-called Amazon women's army of Dahomey, West Africa, used bow-and-arrows in fighting France in 1892. Among the more sporting and well-known of early women archers was Queen Victoria (1837–1901), who learned to handle the bow and arrow as all British monarchs had done before her. Archery has flourished as a sport in Europe since the mid-17th century. The first British national archery championships were held at York in 1844, and the record for longest reign by any British sports champion is still 41 years by archer Alice Blanche Legh (1855–1948), who first won the national championship in 1881 and succeeded in capturing the title a total of 23 times, her final championship coming in 1922, when she was 67 years old.

Archery events for women were included on the Olympic program for the 1904 Games in St. Louis, but only American archers competed, with M. Howell winning both individual gold medals. The Olympics of 1908 and 1920 also included archery events for women, but the sport was then dropped from the program for 52 years, revived only in the 1972 Games at Munich.

Serious international competition began in 1931 with the formation of the Federation Internationale de Tir a l'Arc (FITA), which began with eight member nations and continues to serve as the governing body for the sport. The first FITA World Championship Tournaments, with separate competitions for men and women, were held in Poland in 1931, and were held annually after that until 1959, when they became biennial.

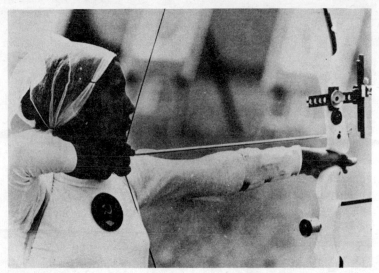

Zebiniso Rustamova scored 1,304 points out of a possible 1,440 in October, 1977.

Competition

World championships are determined on the basis of the top scores in two FITA rounds. In women's archery each round consists of 36 arrows at each of four distances: 70, 60, 50 and 30 meters. The targets are broken up into 5 concentric colored circles, and each color is then divided into two zones, so that each shot is scored from 1 to 10 points. Thus, for each 144-shot round, the highest possible score is 1,440 points.

The pull required to take the string back the length of the arrow, also known as the draw-weight or the weight of the bow, is generally between 24–28 lb. for women (versus 35–45 lb. for men).

Highest Scores

The women's world record score for a single FITA round is 1,304 points by Zebiniso Rustamova (U.S.S.R.) at Milan, Italy, on October 3, 1977.

There are no official world records for Double FITA rounds, but the highest scores achieved in either a world or Olympic championship by a woman is 2,515 points by Luann Ryon (U.S.) at Canberra, Australia, on February 11–12, 1977.

Most World Titles

The greatest number of world archery titles won by a man or woman is seven by Janina Spychajowa-Kurkowska (Poland), who retained the title for the first four years of competition, 1931–34, and won again in 1936, 1939 and 1947.

World Championship—Individual

Year	Winner	Points
1931	Janina Spychajowa-Kurkowska, Poland	—
1932	Janina Spychajowa-Kurkowska, Poland	—
1933	Janina Spychajowa-Kurkowska, Poland	942
1934	Janina Spychajowa-Kurkowska, Poland	867
1935	Ina Catani, Sweden	332
1936	Janina Spychajowa-Kurkowska, Poland	1,875
1937	Erna Simon, G.B.	1,776
1938	Norah Weston-Martyr, G.B., and Louise Nettleton, G.B. (tie)	1,973
1939	Janina Spychajowa-Kurkowska, Poland	2,087
1940–45	No competition	
1946	Petronilla de Wharton Burr, G.B.	1,922
1947	Janina Spychajowa-Kurkowska, Poland	2,321
1948	Petronilla de Wharton Burr, G.B.	2,506
1949	Barbara Waterhouse, G.B.	2,605
1950	Jean Lee, U.S.	3,254
1951	No competition	
1952	Jean Lee, U.S.	3,185
1953	Jean Richards, U.S.	3,056
1954	No competition	
1955	Katarzyna Wisniowska, Poland	3,033
1956	No competition	
1957	Carole Meinhart, U.S.	2,120
1958	Sigrid Johansson, Sweden	2,053
1959	Ann Weber Corby, U.S.	2,023
1961	Nancy Vonderheide, U.S.	2,173
1963	Victoria Cook, U.S.	2,253
1965	Marie Lindholm, Finland	2,214
1967	Maria Maczynska, Poland	2,240
1969	Dorothy Lidstone, Canada	2,361
1971	Emma Gapchenko, U.S.S.R.	2,380
1973	Linda Myers, U.S.	2,204
1975	Zebiniso Rustamova, U.S.S.R.	2,465
1977	Luann Ryon, U.S.	2,515

Team Championship

1933	Poland	1949	Great Britain	1961	U.S.
1934	Poland	1950	Finland	1963	U.S.
1935	Great Britain	1951	No competition	1965	U.S.
1936	Poland	1952	U.S.	1967	Poland
1937	Great Britain	1953	Finland	1969	U.S.S.R.
1938	Poland	1954	No competition	1971	Poland
1939	Poland	1955	Great Britain	1973	U.S.S.R.
1940–45	No competition	1956	No competition	1975	U.S.S.R.
1946	Great Britain	1957	U.S.	1977	U.S.
1947	Denmark	1958	U.S.		
1948	Czechoslovakia	1959	U.S.		

U.S. Championship

Though archery was first introduced as a sport in the U.S. as early as the 17th century, it did not achieve great popularity until the mid-1800's. National championships for men and women began in 1879 with the formation of the National Archery Association, which is still the governing body for the sport in the U.S. The first national championship meeting took place in Chicago in August, 1879, where 20 women and 69 men competed. The women's title that year was won by Mrs. S. Brown.

Competition

Women's target competition for the U.S. Championship includes two types of round. The National Round, the basis for the first U.S. Championships, consists of 48 arrows shot at a distance of 60 yards and 24 arrows shot at 50 yards. For the Columbia Round, archers shoot 24 arrows at each of three distances, 50, 40 and 30 yards. From 1879 through 1909 the National Round alone determined the women's champion. From 1910 through 1914 there were separate National Round and Columbia Round champions, and since 1915 the championship has been determined by the total score in two National and two Columbia Rounds.

Most Titles

The most successful woman archer in U.S. National competition has been Mrs. M. C. Howell, who won the title 17 times, in 1883, 85, 86, 90–93, 95, 96, 98–1900, 02–05, 07. She also won the gold medals in both the Columbia and National Rounds in the first Olympic archery competition, at the 1904 Games in St. Louis.

Olympic

Archery competition has been included in the 1972 and 1976 Games, and is on the program for the 1980 Games in Moscow. The medal winners to date are as follows:

	Gold	*Silver*	*Bronze*
1972	Doreen Wilbur (U.S.) 2,424 pts.	Irena Szydlwska (Pol.) 2,407	Emma Gapchenko (U.S.S.R.) 2,403
1976	Luann Ryon (U.S.) 2,499 pts.	Valentina Kovpan (U.S.S.R.) 2,460	Zebiniso Rustamova (U.S.S.R.) 2,407

Flight Shooting

In flight shooting competition there is no target—the archers aim for distance only. The current women's record is 810 yards 1 foot 9 inches by April Moon (U.S.) at Wendover, Utah, on September 17, 1977.

Auto Racing

Land Speed Record

The highest land speed recorded by a woman is 524.016 m.p.h. by Kitty O'Neil (born 1948 in Texas). Strapped into the 48,000-h.p. rocket-powered 3-wheeled S.M.I. *Motivator* weighing 4,949 lb. and stretching $38\frac{1}{2}$ feet in length, O'Neil sped across the Alvard Desert in Oregon on December 6, 1976. Her official 2-way record was 512.710 m.p.h., and she probably reached 600 m.p.h. momentarily.

Kitty O'Neil has displayed her courage on land, water and in the air, setting speed records as a sportswoman and plunging from enormous heights as a stuntwoman.

Kitty O'Neil (now Mrs. Hambleton) has overcome enormous obstacles to reach her present position as a top Hollywood stuntwoman and world record holder. She was born deaf, yet with the help of her Cherokee Indian mother and Irish father, she learned to read lips and set out to search for challenges which would belie her "handicapped" state. In her daring stunt career she has been set on fire and has plunged from a 125-foot cliff. She has excelled on the water as well as on land, winning 86 first-place trophies as an amateur diver and at one time holding the record as the fastest woman on water skis. While she was training for an attempt at a berth on the 1964 U.S. Olympic diving team, doctors informed her that she was suffering from spinal meningitis, and would probably be paralyzed for life. She fought back, and despite the diagnosis nearly qualified for the Olympic team, and went on to set new marks for automotive speed. She is still actively striving to set new records in land and water vehicles.

First Women Racers

Automobile racing began in 1878 with a 201-mile competition from Green Bay, to Madison, Wisconsin, between steam-powered vehicles. The first successful gasoline-driven car was built by Karl-Friedrich Benz in late 1885 in Germany, and the first major race was run from Paris to Bordeaux and back again on June 11–13, 1895.

Dorothy Levitt (right) was the leading woman racer in the early 1900's, and her book helped to popularize motoring for the everyday woman driver. Gwenda Stewart (below) is seen here at Brooklands Track in her Derby-Miller car.

The first woman auto racer was Madame Laumaille, who finished fourth in a two-day run from Marseilles to Nice in 1898. Her husband finished sixth. The first American woman race driver was somewhat less successful. Racing in New York City in 1899, Genevra Delphine Mudge knocked down five spectators in her Locomobile before stalling in the snow.

Dorothy Levitt was the premier woman race driver at the turn of the century. In 1905 she won a road race at Brighton, setting a woman's world speed record of 79¾ m.p.h. In 1906 she raised this mark to 91 m.p.h. She participated in one of the first road rallies, the Herkomer Trophy Race, held in Germany in 1907, finishing fourth out of 172 competitors of both sexes. In addition to her outstanding performance behind the wheel, she was the first woman to succeed as a motorboat racer, winning her first race at Cowes, England, in 1903. In 1906 she wrote a book of advice for lady motorists called *The Woman and the Car.*

Gwenda Stewart began her racing career on a motorcycle, which she learned to ride at age 15. After compiling an impressive service record driving an ambulance and heavy trucks in World War I, she returned to motorcycle racing, but a serious crash in 1927 led her to concentrate instead on automobile competition. At one time she held 76 records, including several at the famed Montlhéry Racetrack in France, where she was one of three women out of 74 drivers to receive special badges for record holders, awarded by racing authorities. Driving a 1,673-c.c. supercharged Derby-Miller in 1935, Stewart set a record for the up-to-2-liter automobile class with her extraordinary 135.95 lap on the outer circuit at Brooklands Track in England. This led officials to discontinue the ladies' championship there (begun in 1928) in the belief that speeds of this magnitude were too hazardous for women drivers.

Janet Guthrie, the first woman at Indy, waves happily to the crowd after her ninth place finish in the 1978 race.

Indianapolis 500

The first and only woman to qualify for and compete in the prestigious Indianapolis 500-mile race (first run on May 30, 1911) is Janet Guthrie (born 1937). She passed her rookie test in May, 1976, and earned the right to compete in the qualifying rounds, but was unable to win a place on the starting line when the Vollstedt-Offenhauser she drove was withdrawn from the race after repeated mechanical failures.

Despite this setback, Guthrie succeeded in setting a record in May, 1976. She moved on quickly to Charlotte, North Carolina, where she entered the World 600. She drove her Chevy to 15th place out of 40 entrants to become the first woman to drive in a major stock car race.

In the 61st running of the Indianapolis 500, in 1977, Guthrie became the first woman to compete, although her car developed mechanical problems which forced her to retire after 27 laps. In 1978, she completed the race, finishing in ninth place after 190 laps.

Grand Prix

The first woman to drive in a world championship Grand Prix race was Maria Teresa de Fillipis (Italy), in the Belgian Grand Prix at Spa on June 15, 1958. She finished in tenth place driving a Maserati.

The first woman to actually score in the world championship table was Lella Lombardi (Italy, born March 26, 1943), when she was awarded ½ point for her sixth position in the 1975 Spanish Grand Prix at Barcelona, which was stopped prematurely due to an accident, leading to the halving of the points awarded.

Drag Racing

Terminal velocity in drag racing is the speed attained at the end of a 440-yard run made from a standing start, and the world record for the fastest terminal velocity is held by a woman, Shirley "Cha-Cha" Muldowney, who recorded a speed of 252.10 m.p.h. in OCIR competition on January 15, 1977, at Beeline Drag Strip, Phoenix, Arizona. Later that year she turned in an even faster time, 253.52 m.p.h. on May 7 at Orange County International Raceway (California), but this record remained unofficial when bad weather washed out her opportunity to fulfill the National Hot Rod Association requirement of another run within one per cent of the record run before certification.

Shirley Muldowney became the first woman to qualify to drive top fuel dragsters in 1975, at age 35.

Along with her world speed record, she holds a number of impressive "firsts," beginning with the fact that she is the first and only woman in the U.S. licensed to drive top fuel dragsters. She was also the first woman ever to drive a quarter mile in under 6 seconds (her best is 5.77 seconds), and the first woman to win at the N.H.R.A. Spring Nationals with her victory in 1976, a title she captured again in 1977.

Road Rallies

The most successful woman in rally events has been Pat Moss, who boasts an impressive string of victories over male competitors in major international races. Her greatest victory came in 1960, winning the Liége-Rome-Liége rally with Anne Wisdom in an Austin Healey 3000. Other major wins came in 1962 in the Tulip and German Rallies (driving a Mini Cooper) and the Sestrière Rally (in a Lancia Fulvia).

Long Distance Driving

Violet Cordery was the first woman to drive around the world, completing a 10,266-mile journey through five continents in 1927. She averaged just over 24 m.p.h. in her 3-liter Invicta.

Paula Murphy (*née* Mulhauser) drove 26,412.20 miles in the U.S. Bicentennial Global Record Run, from July 4-October 15, 1976, in a Pontiac Sunbird, finishing in 105 days 2 hours 29 minutes 25.0 seconds. Gasoline purchased on the trip through 28 countries varied from 18¢ to $2.00 a gallon.

Badminton

In the early 1870's British army officers brought the rudiments of the game with them from India, where it was called "Poona." They introduced it at Badminton Hall in Avon, England, which gave the game its modern name. By 1887 the rules had been standardized, and in 1899 the first All-England Championships were held for men and women. This remained the premier tournament in the world until World Championships were begun in 1977.

International competition was instituted under the auspices of the International Badminton Federation (founded 1934). The men's championship competition for the Thomas Cup was first held in November, 1948. Women's competition for the Uber Cup began in March, 1957, with a victory for the U.S. team. Since then the Uber Cup matches have been played every three years.

Competition

The equipment and court layout are the same for men and women. In women's single play, a game is 11 points (for men it is 15 points). In all other respects the rules are the same for both sexes, in singles and doubles play. Matches are won by the first player or team to win two out of three games.

All-England Championships —Women's Singles

1899	No competition	1905	Mary Lucas
1900	Ethel Thomson	1906	Ethel Thomson
1901	Ethel Thomson	1907	Mary Lucas
1902	Mary Lucas	1908	Mary Lucas
1903	Ethel Thomson	1909	Mary Lucas
1904	Ethel Thomson	1910	Mary Lucas

1911	Margaret Lamine
1912	Margaret Tragett
1913	Lavinia Radeglia
1914	Lavinia Radeglia
1915–19	No competition
1920	Kathleen McKane
1921	Kathleen McKane
1922	Kathleen McKane
1923	Lavinia Radeglia
1924	Kathleen McKane
1925	Margaret McKane Stocks
1926	Marjorie Barrett
1927	Marjorie Barrett
1928	Marjorie Barrett
1929	Marjorie Barrett
1930	Marjorie Barrett
1931	Marjorie Barrett
1932	Leonie Kingsbury
1933	Alice Woodroffe
1934	Leonie Kingsbury
1935	Betty Uber
1936	Thelma Kingsbury
1937	Thelma Kingsbury
1938	Daphne Young
1939	Dorothy Walton
1940–46	No competition
1947	Marie Ussing
1948	Kirsten Thorndahl
1949	Aase Schiött Jacobsen
1950	Tonny Olsen Ahm
1951	Aase Schiött Jacobsen
1952	Tonny Olsen Ahm
1953	Marie Ussing
1954	Judith Devlin
1955	Margaret Varner
1956	Margaret Varner
1957	Judith Devlin
1958	Judith Devlin
1959	Heather Ward
1960	Judith Devlin
1961	Judith Devlin Hashman
1962	Judith Devlin Hashman
1963	Judith Devlin Hashman
1964	Judith Devlin Hashman
1965	Ursula Smith
1966	Judith Devlin Hashman
1967	Judith Devlin Hashman
1968	Eva Twedberg

Judy Devlin Hashman won 17 All-England Championships and 32 U.S. titles.

1969	Hiroe Yuki
1970	Etsuko Takenaka
1971	Eva Twedberg
1972	Noriko Takagi Nakayama
1973	Margaret Beck
1974	Hiroe Yuki
1975	Hiroe Yuki
1976	Gillian Gilks
1977	Hiroe Yuki
1978	Gillian Gilks

Women's Doubles

1899	Mary Lucas—Miss Graeme
1900	Mary Lucas—Miss Graeme
1901	Miss St. John—E. M. Moseley
1902	Mary Lucas—Ethel Thomson
1903	M. Hardy—Dorothea Douglass
1904	Mary Lucas—Ethel Thomson
1905	Mary Lucas—Ethel Thomson
1906	Mary Lucas—Ethel Thomson
1907	Mary Lucas—G. L. Murray
1908	Mary Lucas—G. L. Murray
1909	Mary Lucas—G. L. Murray
1910	Mary Bateman—Mary Lucas
1911	A. Gowenlock—Dorothy Cundall
1912	A. Gowenlock—Dorothy Cundall
1913	Hazel Hogarth—Mary Bateman
1914	Margaret Tragett—Eveline Peterson
1915–19	No competition
1920	Lavinia Radeglia—Violet Elton
1921	Kathleen McKane—Margaret McKane
1922	Margaret Tragett—Hazel Hogarth
1923	Margaret Tragett—Hazel Hogarth
1924	Margaret McKane Stocks—Kathleen McKane
1925	Margaret Tragett—Hazel Hogarth
1926	A. M. Head—Violet Elton
1927	Margaret Tragett—Hazel Hogarth
1928	Marjorie Barrett—Violet Elton
1929	Marjorie Barrett—Violet Elton
1930	Marjorie Barrett—Violet Elton
1931	Betty Uber—Marianne Horsley
1932	Marjorie Barrett—Leonie Kingsbury
1933	Thelma Kingsbury—Marjorie Bell
1934	Thelma Kingsbury—Marjorie Bell Henderson
1935	Thelma Kingsbury—Marjorie Bell Henderson
1936	Thelma Kingsbury—Marjorie Bell Henderson
1937	Betty Uber—Diana Doveton
1938	Betty Uber—Diana Doveton
1939	Ruth Dalsgard—Tonny Olsen
1940–46	No competition
1947	Tonny Olsen Ahm—Kirsten Thorndahl
1948	Tonny Olsen Ahm—Kirsten Thorndahl
1949	Betty Uber—Queenie Allen
1950	Tonny Olsen Ahm—Kirsten Thorndahl
1951	Tonny Olsen Ahm—Kirsten Thorndahl
1952	Tonny Olsen Ahm—Aase Schiött Jacobsen
1953	Iris L. Cooley—June R. White
1954	Judith Devlin—Susan Devlin

1955	Iris L. Cooley—June R. White
1956	Judith Devlin—Susan Devlin
1957	Kirsten Thorndahl Grandlund—Ami Hammergard
1958	Margaret Varner—Heather Ward
1959	Iris Cooley Rogers—June White Timperley
1960	Judith Devlin—Susan Devlin
1961	Judith Devlin Hashman—Susan Devlin Peard
1962	Judith Devlin Hashman—T. Holst-Christensen
1963	Judith Devlin Hashman—Susan Devlin Peard
1964	Karen Jorgensen—Ulla Rasmussen
1965	Karen Jorgensen—Ulla Rasmussen Strand
1966	Judith Devlin Hashman—Susan Devlin Peard
1967	Imre Rietveld—Ulla Rasmussen Strand
1968	Miss Minarni—Retno Koestijah
1969	Margaret Boxall—Susan Whetnall
1970	Margaret Boxall—Susan Whetnall
1971	Noriko Takagi—Hiroe Yuki
1972	Machiko Aizawa—Etsuko Takenaka
1973	Machiko Aizawa—Etsuko Takenaka
1974	Margaret Beck—Gillian Gilks
1975	Machiko Aizawa—Etsuko Takenaka
1976	Gillian Gilks—Susan Whetnall
1977	Etsuko Toganoo—Eruko Ueno
1978	Atsuko Tokuda—Mikiko Takada

Ladies International Championship (Uber Cup)

The trophy for the ladies' tournament was presented by Betty (Mrs. H. S.) Uber, herself a four-time winner in the All-England Championships (singles in 1935, doubles in 1931, 37 and 49). The most successful nation has been Japan, winning the trophy four times. The only nation to hold both the men's and women's championships simultaneously has been Indonesia, in 1975.

Uber Cup Winners

1956–57   United States
   Defeated Denmark 6-1 in England
1959–60   United States
   Defeated Denmark 5-2 at Philadelphia, Pa.

1962–63   United States
Defeated England 4-3 at Wilmington, Del.
1965–66   Japan
Defeated United States 5-2 at Wellington, New Zealand
1968–69   Japan
Defeated Indonesia 6-1 at Tokyo, Japan
1971–72   Japan
Defeated Indonesia 6-1 at Tokyo, Japan
1974–75   Indonesia
Defeated Japan 5-2 at Jakarta, Indonesia
1977–78   Japan
Defeated Indonesia 5-2 in New Zealand

Most Titles

Judy Devlin Hashman (U.S., born 1935) is the most accomplished woman badminton player of all time. She holds the record for singles wins in the All-England Championship with 10 (the greatest number by a man is 8 by Rudy Hartono of Indonesia). She shares the record of 17 total wins, including doubles, with Mary Lucas.

In addition to her English triumphs she has won 12 U.S. singles titles (1954, 56–63, 65–67), 12 U.S. doubles titles (1953–55, 57–63, 66, 67), including ten paired with her sister Susan, and 8 U.S. mixed doubles titles (1956–62, 67).

Shortest Game

In the 1969 Uber Cup competition, Noriko Takagi (later Mrs. Nakayama) of Japan defeated P. Tumengkol in 9 minutes.

Marathon

The record for a member of either sex playing continuous singles against a number of different opponents is 72 hours 17 minutes by Karen Haubrich of La Jolla, California, on August 17–20, 1977.

Basketball

The game of "Pok-ta-Pok" was played in the 10th century B.C. by the Olmecs in Mexico, and closely resembled basketball in its concept. "Ollamalitzli" was a variation of this game played by the Aztecs in Mexico as late as the 16th century. If the solid rubber ball was put through a fixed stone ring, the player was entitled to the clothing of all the spectators.

Modern basketball was devised by the Canadian-born Dr. James A. Naismith (1861–1939) at the Training School of the International Y.M.C.A. College at Springfield, Massachusetts, in mid-December, 1891. The first women basketball players were teachers from the Buckingham Grade School in Springfield who were taught the game by Naismith at the Y.M.C.A. College gym soon after he had invented it. Women at Smith College in Northampton, Massachusetts, began playing the game in 1892.

In 1895, Clara Baer of Newcomb College, New Orleans, Louisiana, published an influential set of rules for women's basketball. The rules have been revised and altered repeatedly, and there continues to be a split between those who adhere to the old-style team formation, with six players on a team and only three allowed to score, and the more popular five-woman team, with rules essentially the same as in men's basketball.

International women's amateur championship competition began in 1953 under the auspices of the International Basketball Federation (the F.I.B.A., founded 1932). The first Olympic competition for women was included in the 1976 Games at Montreal, with the Russian women defeating the U.S. for the gold medal in the finals.

Olympic Games

In the only Olympic basketball competion held so far, in 1976, the gold medal went to the Russian team, the silver to the U.S. and the bronze to Bulgaria. The Russian team consisted of the following 12 players:

Angele Rupshene	Iuliana Semenova
Tatyana Zakharova	Nadyezhda Zakharova
Raisa Kurvyakova	Nelli Feryabnikova
Olga Barisheva	Olga Sukharnova
Tatyana Ovetchkina	Tamara Daunene
Nadyezhda Shuvayeva	Natalia Klimova

Women's World Amateur Championship

1953	U.S.	1967	U.S.S.R.
1957	U.S.	1971	U.S.S.R.
1959	U.S.S.R.	1975	U.S.S.R.
1964	U.S.S.R.		

Highest International Score

The highest score by a women's team in an international match is 153 by the U.S.S.R. against Switzerland (who scored 25 points) on June 4, 1956, in the European Championships.

Tallest Player

The tallest woman player is Iuliana Semenova (born 1951), star center for the indomitable Russian team. She reputedly stands 7 feet 2 inches tall and weighs 281 lb.

A.A.U. National Championship

The National A.A.U. Women's Basketball Championship was instituted in 1926, when the Pasadena A. and C.C. team from California won the title. Since that time the most successful entry has been the team from Plainview, Texas, which under the names Wayland Flying Queens, Hutcherson Flying Queens and, most recently, Wayland College, has won the championship 10 times (1954–57, 59, 61, 70–71, 74–75).

Billiards

The earliest recorded mention of billiards was in France in 1429, and it was mentioned in England in 1588 in inventories of the Duke of Norfolk's Howard House and the Earl of Leicester's property in Essex. The first recorded public room for billiards in England, was the Piazza Covent Garden, London, in the early part of the 19th century. Rubber cushions were introduced on billiard tables in 1835, and slate beds in 1836.

Women have long been interested in the game, although formal championship competition has been sparse. It is reported that Mary, Queen of Scots, complained during her captivity in 1576 that her billiard table had been taken away.

Most Amateur Titles

The record number of women's amateur titles is nine, achieved by Maureen Barrett Baynton between 1955 and 1968, and Vera Selby from 1970 to 1978.

Pocket Billiards Championship

Jean Balukas of Brooklyn, New York (born 1959) has won the U.S. Open Pocket Billiards Championship a record seven times, with consecutive wins from 1972–78. She won her first championship, which carried a $1,500 first prize, when she was 14 years old.

Bowling

Bowling can be traced to articles found in the tomb of an Egyptian child of 5200 B.C., where there were nine pieces of stone to be set up as pins at which a stone "ball" was rolled. There is also a resemblance to a Polynesian game called *ula maika* which utilized pins and balls of stone. The stones were rolled a distance of 60 feet. In the Italian Alps about 2,000 years ago, the underhand tossing of stones at an object is believed to be the beginnings of *bocci*, a game still widely played in Italy.

Bowling at pins probably originated in ancient Germany as a religious ceremony. Martin Luther is credited with the statement that nine was the ideal number of pins. In the British Isles, lawn bowls was preferred to bowling at pins, but in the 16th century, bowling at pins was the national sport of Scotland.

How bowling at pins came to the United States is a matter of controversy. Early British settlers probably brought lawn bowls and set up what is known as Bowling Green at the tip of Manhattan Island in New York, but perhaps the Dutch under Henry Hudson were the ones to be credited. Some historians say that in Connecticut the tenth pin was added to evade a legal ban against nine-pin bowling in 1845, but others say that ten pins was played in New York City before this date and point to Washington Irving's "Rip Van Winkle," written about 1818, as evidence.

After two unsuccessful attempts at setting up national organizations to supervise bowling competition, the American Bowling Congress was founded in 1895, organizing its first national tournament for men in 1901. In 1916, the Women's International Bowling Congress was formed (originally called the Women's National Bowling Association). Women held their first tournament in St. Louis, Mo., with eight teams competing, along with 16 doubles entries and 24 singles. The total prize fund was $222.00. Today the W.I.B.C. has become the largest sports organization for women in the world, with sanctioned members totaling 4,209,220 in 1978. The Professional Women's Bowling Association was founded in 1959, making it the first professional women's sports organization in the United States.

Bev Ortner rolled games of 267, 264 and 287 to achieve her record 818 series on October 10, 1968.

WOMEN'S INTERNATIONAL BOWLING CONGRESS RECORDS

All-Time Records, League Play

Highest Series

The highest individual score for three games is 818 by Bev Ortner (now of Tucson, Arizona) in Galva, Iowa, in 1968. The highest team score is 3,379 by Freeway Washer of Cleveland, Ohio, in 1960.

Consecutive Strikes, Consecutive Spares

The record for consecutive strikes in sanctioned play is 18 by Georgene Cordes of Bloomington, Minnesota, rolled during the 1970–71 season. The most spares in a row is 27 by Joan Taylor of Syracuse, New York, during the 1973–74 season.

Most Perfect Scores

The greatest number of sanctioned 300 games by a woman in

Dorothy Miller won 10 W.I.B.C. Championships in a 20-year period, including six team championships.

a career is five, rolled by Betty Morris of Stockton, California. She also holds the record for the most 700-plus series in a career, with 51.

Most Consecutive 600 Series

Maureen Harris of Madison, Wisconsin, bowled 22 consecutive 600-point three-game series between November 30, 1970, and April 26, 1971. Six of these series were in the 700's.

Marathons

Frieda Wood of Fort Worth, Texas, bowled for 72 hours 13 minutes on January 30, 1973, completing 147 games. Bonnie Benton of Miami, Florida, bowled for a longer time, 132 hours, but rolled one less game, with 146, in July, 1977.

W.I.B.C. Tournament Records

The W.I.B.C. Championships are held each year, with competition for four titles: all-events, singles, doubles, and five-woman team.

Most Championship Titles

Dorothy Miller of Chicago, Illinois, a member of the W.I.B.C. Hall of Fame, won the most championships with 10 between 1928 and 1948, three of which were won consecutively.

Best Finishes in One Tournament

Four W.I.B.C. members have succeeded in winning three championship titles in a single tournament. A. J. Koester of St. Louis and Dorothy Fothergill of North Attleboro, Massachusetts, won the singles, the all-events, and were on the winning team in 1916 and 1970, respectively. Tess Small of Chicago and Doris Knechtges of Detroit won the all-events, the doubles and were on the winning team in 1940 and 1953, respectively.

Highest Series

The highest three-game series total is 737 by D. D. Jacobson of Playa Del Rey, California, in the 1972 singles event. Dorothy Fothergill of North Attleboro, Massachusetts, holds the nine-game all-events record of 1,984, set in 1970.

Highest Doubles Score

Marge Merrick and Elizabeth Miller of Columbus, Ohio, turned in a record 504 in the 1962 doubles event. The record score for a doubles pair in a three-game series is 1,315 by Gloria Simon of Portland, Oregon, and Judy Soutar of Kansas City, Missouri.

Highest Single Game

There has never been a perfect game bowled in the W.I.B.C. tournament. The highest individual score has been a 296, rolled by Martha Hoffman, of Madison, Wisconsin, in the 1962 singles event.

Most Team Entries

The greatest number of five-person teams entered in a single tournament in either men's or women's competition has been 9,688 women's teams entered in the W.I.B.C. tournament in Milwaukee, Wisconsin in 1977.

Youngest Winner

The youngest champion was Lorrie Nichols of Carpentersville, Illinois, who won the 1971 all-events title at age 19.

Bull Fighting

In the latter half of the second millenium B.C., bull leaping was practiced in Crete. Bull fighting in Spain was first reported by the Romans in Baetica (Andalusia) in the third century B.C. The first written mention of a *torera* (a woman bull fighter) appeared in 1654. The great Spanish artist Francisco Goya (1746–1828), who designed a uniform for matadors to be worn at *corridas* on gala occasions, depicted a *torera* called "La Pajuelera" in action in one of his paintings.

Spain now has some 190 active matadors. The most famous female bullfighter presently is Maribel Atienzar, known to her fans as "Gentle Maribel," who began her career at the age of 14. By the time she was 17 she had killed 35 bulls.

Early *Toreras*

Women have been active in the *corrida* since at least the 17th century, usually on horseback. The first woman to achieve major success in modern times was Conchita Cintrón (born 1922). She appeared in Latin America and in Spain, starting on horseback at the age of 12. Her first appearance on foot as a *torera* came at age 15 in Mexico, and by the age of 21 she had killed 400 bulls on foot. She opened the way for female bull fighters throughout South America, Spain and Portugal in a career which spanned over 25 years. She has led a full and varied life since her retirement from the ring, finding success as a dog breeder, diplomatic attaché, writer and mother.

Bull fighting by women on foot was banned in Spain from 1908 to 1973. The first woman to appear as a *torera* after the ban was lifted was Maria de Los Angeles.

The first native American woman to be a professional bull fighter was Patricia McCormick, who made her debut in Ciudad Juarez, Mexico, on January 20, 1952. Conchita Cintrón had American parents, but was born in Chile and raised in Peru.

Canoeing

The canoe has existed for centuries as a means of transportation, but the acknowledged pioneer of canoeing as a sport was John Macgregor, a British barrister, in 1865.

Women's world championship competition began with the kayak singles event in 1938, conducted under the auspices of the International Representationschaft des Kanusport (founded 1924). The competition lapsed for 10 years, and was renewed with the first women's Olympic canoeing competition, at the 1948 Games in London. Since that time championships have been held under the supervision of the International Canoe Federation (I.C.F.), founded in 1945, which took over as governing body for the sport when the I.R.K. dissolved during World War II.

The championships were held every two years (including the Olympic events) until 1970, when they were made annual. In addition to the kayak singles (K-1) event, the kayak pairs (K-2) and kayak fours (K-4) are now contested in the world championships, each raced over a 500-meter course, along with a K-1 slalom title. In the Olympic Games there are only two women's categories, K-1 and K-2. A slalom event was included in 1972, but subsequently dropped.

World Championships

Kayak Singles (K-1)   *Asterisk indicates Olympic title*

1938 Maggie Kalka, Finland	1960* Antonina Seredina, U.S.S.R.
1948* Karen Hoff, Denmark	
1950 Sylvi Saimo, Finland	1963 Maria Zhubina, U.S.S.R.
1952* Sylvi Saimo, Finland	1964* Ludmila Khvedosyuk, U.S.S.R.
1954 Therese Zenz, Germany	
1956 Elisaveta Dementyeva, U.S.S.R.	1966 Ludmila Pinayeva (*née* Khvedosyuk), U.S.S.R.
1958 Elisaveta Kislova, U.S.S.R.	

1968* Ludmila Pinayeva, U.S.S.R.
1970 Ludmila Pinayeva, U.S.S.R.
1971 Ludmila Pinayeva, U.S.S.R.
1972* Julia Ryabchinskaya, U.S.S.R.

1973 Nina Gopova, U.S.S.R.
1974 Anke Ohde, E. Germany
1975 Anke Ohde, E. Germany
1976* Carola Zirzow, E. Germany
1977 G. Dittmar, E. Germany
1978 Roswitha Eberl, E. Germany

Nina Gopova and Galina Kreft won the 1976 K-2 title with a time of 1 minute 51.15 seconds for 500 meters.

Kayak Pairs (K-2)

1938 Marta Pavlisova—Marta Zvolankova, Czech.
1948 Karen Hoff—Sventsen, Denmark
1950 Sylvi Saimo—Grönholm, Finland
1952 No competition
1954 Pinter—Klára Bánfalvi, Hungary
1956 No competition
1958 Maria Zhubina—Nina Gruzintseva, U.S.S.R.
1960* Maria Zhubina—Antonina Seredina, U.S.S.R.
1963 Annemarie Zimmermann—Roswitha Esser, W. Germany
1964* Annemarie Zimmermann—Roswitha Esser, W. Germany
1966 Anita Kobuss—H. Ulze, E. Germany
1968* Annemarie Zimmermann—Roswitha Esser, W. Germany
1970 Renate Breuer—Roswitha Esser, W. Germany
1971 Anna Pfeffer—Katalin Höllösy, Hungary
1972* Ludmila Pinayeva—Ekaterina Kuryshko, U.S.S.R.
1973 Ilse Kaschube—Petra Borzym, E. Germany
1974 Anke Ohde—Barbel Koster, E. Germany
1975 Barbel Koster—Carola Zirzow, E. Germany
1976* Nina Gopova—Galina Kreft, U.S.S.R.
1977 Marion Rösiger—Martina Fischer, E. Germany
1978 Marion Rösiger—Martina Fischer, E. Germany

Kayak Fours (K-4)

1966	U.S.S.R.	1974	E. Germany
1970	U.S.S.R.	1975	E. Germany
1971	U.S.S.R.	1977	Bulgaria
1973	U.S.S.R.	1978	E. Germany

Slalom K-1

1949	Heidi Pillwein, Austria	1967	Ludmila Polesná, Czech.
1951	Gerti Pertlweiser, Austria	1969	Ludmila Polesná, Czech.
1953	Fritzi Schwingl, Austria	1971	Angelika Bahmann, E. Germany
1955	Rosemarie Bisinger, W. Germany	1972*	Angelika Bahmann, E. Germany
1957	Brigitte Magnus, E. Germany	1973	Sybille Spindler, E. Germany
1959	Hilde Urbaniak, W. Germany	1975	Maria Cwiertniewicz, Poland
1961	Ludmila Veberova, U.S.S.R.	1977	Angelika Bahmann, E. Germany
1963	Ludmila Veberova, U.S.S.R.		
1965	Ursula Gläser, E. Germany		

Most Titles

Ludmila Pinayeva (*née* Khvedosyuk) is the foremost record holder in canoeing. She won a record three Olympic gold medals and six world championship titles between 1966 and 1973 in K-1, K-2 and K-4 events.

Long Distance Canoeing

Women have figured in the crews of at least two of the major distance canoeing record journeys. John and Julie Batchelor of Great Britain conquered the Congo River in record time, traveling the 2,600 miles from Moasampanga to Banana in 128 days, from May 8–September 12, 1974.

Beatrice Dowd was a member of the four-person crew (John Dowd, Ken Beard and Steve Benson, who was replaced in mid-journey by Richard Gillet, were her male compatriots) which completed the longest open sea voyage ever undertaken by

The crew for the longest open sea canoe voyage was (left to right) John Dowd, Beatrice Dowd, Stephen Benson and Kenneth Beard.

canoe. They set out in two Klepper Aerius 20 kayaks on August 11, 1977, from Venezuela, and traveled 1,559 miles to reach Miami, Florida on April 29, 1978.

National Women's Championships

The American Canoe Association (founded in 1880), in addition to choosing the teams which compete for the U.S. in the Olympic canoeing competition, conducts the annual women's national championships in K-1, K-2 and K-4. The most successful participant to date has been Marcia Jones Smoke, who won a total of 33 national championships, including 11 K-1 titles (1963–73, tied with her sister, Sperry Jones Rademaker, in 1965), 8 K-2 titles (1962 with Eileen Murphy, 1966–70 and 1972 with Sperry Jones Rademaker, 1971 with Kathy Mosolino) and 10 K-4 titles (1962, 63, 66–68, 70–73, 76). She is also an Olympic medalist, with the bronze in the K-1 event in 1964.

Croquet

Croquet, in its present-day form, originated as a country-house lawn game in Ireland in the 1830's, when it was called "crokey." The game enjoyed tremendous popularity from the 1870's–1890's as a pleasant outdoor game which could be enjoyed by both sexes. With the widespread acceptance of lawn tennis at the turn of the century, however, croquet lost most of its followers as an organized sport. A related game called "roque" was invented in the U.S. at about this time, played on a hard surface and emphasizing greater accuracy and skill. The American Roque League (founded 1916), though, has never accepted women as members, and does not to the present day.

The game of croquet is still played competitively, in marked different forms, in both England and the U.S. For English Croquet the major tournaments are the Open Croquet Championships (instituted 1867), the Men's Championship and the Women's Championship.

Dorothy Dyne Steel regularly defeated both male and female opponents throughout a career spanning more than 20 years.

Most Titles

Dorothy Dyne Steel (1884–1965) won a total of 31 titles, including the Open Croquet Championship four times (1925,

33, 35, 36), the Women's Championship fifteen times (1919–39), five doubles and seven mixed doubles titles. She also holds the distinction of playing with the lowest handicap for a woman, with minus 5.

Cross-Country Running

Cross-country is generally pursued as a winter sport in which competitors race through the countryside in a predetermined course, the length of which varies according to the local conditions. The earliest recorded international cross-country race took place over 9 miles 8 yards from Ville D'Avray, outside Paris, on March 20, 1898, between England and France. International Championships for women were instituted in 1967, and are now held annually. The course for the women's event varies in distance from $2\frac{1}{2}$ to $3\frac{1}{8}$ miles.

International Championship, Individual

1967 Doris Brown, U.S.	1974 Paola Cacchi, Italy
1968 Doris Brown, U.S.	1975 Julie Brown, U.S.
1969 Doris Brown, U.S.	1976 Carmen Valero Omedes, Spain
1970 Doris Brown, U.S.	
1971 Doris Brown, U.S.	1977 Carmen Valero Omedes, Spain
1972 Joyce Smith, England	
1973 Paola Cacchi, Italy	1978 Grete Waitz, Norway

International Championship, Team

1967 England	1971 England	1975 U.S.
1968 U.S.	1972 England	1976 U.S.S.R.
1969 U.S.	1973 England	1977 U.S.S.R.
1970 England	1974 England	1978 Rumania

Cycling

Beryl Burton was particularly successful in the pursuit event, in which she won the women's title five times.

The first design for a machine propelled by cranks and pedals with connecting rods has been attributed to Leonardo da Vinci or one of his pupils, dated *c.*1493. The first practical bicycle, however, was not built until 1839 or 1840 by Kirkpatrick Macmillan of Dumfries, Scotland. In 1870, Samuel Webb Thomas patented a design for a lady's bicycle, arranged to allow the feminine pedal-pusher to ride sidesaddle.

The earliest recorded bicycle race was a velocipede race over 2 kilometers (1.24 miles) at the Parc de St. Cloud, Paris, on May 31, 1868, won by James Moore of Great Britain. Bicycle racing developed on both the professional and amateur levels in Europe and the U.S., both outdoors and indoors on wooden tracks. In the 1890's, beginning in New York City and spreading through much of the U.S. and Canada, the six-day marathon race became a popular craze, drawing thousands of paying spectators to such arenas as Madison Square Garden in New York City and the Olympia in Detroit. The first such race for women was held from January 6–11, 1896 at Madison Square Garden. Frankie Nelson covered 418 miles to win before a crowd of 4,000 spectators at the finish.

The first women's championship race in the U.S., sanctioned by the National Amateur Bicycling Association was held in Buffalo, New York, on September 4, 1937, and won by Doris Kopsky of Belleville, New Jersey, who completed the mile distance in 4 minutes 22.4 seconds. International women's championships began in 1958.

World Championship

Sprint

1958	Galina Ermolayeva, U.S.S.R.	1967	Valentia Savina, U.S.S.R.
1959	Galina Ermolayeva, U.S.S.R.	1968	Alla Baguiniantz, U.S.S.R.
1960	Galina Ermolayeva, U.S.S.R.	1969	Galina Tsareva, U.S.S.R.
1961	Galina Ermolayeva, U.S.S.R.	1970	Galina Tsareva, U.S.S.R.
1962	Valentia Savina, U.S.S.R.	1971	Galina Tsareva, U.S.S.R.
1963	Galina Ermolayeva, U.S.S.R.	1972	Galina Ermolayeva, U.S.S.R.
1964	Irina Kiritchenko, U.S.S.R.	1973	Sheila Young, U.S.
1965	Valentia Savina, U.S.S.R.	1974	Tamara Piltsikova, U.S.S.R.
1966	Irina Kiritchenko, U.S.S.R.	1975	Sue Novarra, U.S.
		1976	Sheila Young, U.S.
		1977	Galina Tsareva, U.S.S.R.
		1978	Galina Tsareva, U.S.S.R.

Pursuit

1958	Lubov Kotchetova, U.S.S.R.	1965	Yvonne Reynders, Belgium
1959	Beryl Burton, G.B.	1966	Beryl Burton, G.B.
1960	Beryl Burton, G.B.	1967	Tamara Garkuskina, U.S.S.R.
1961	Yvonne Reynders, Belgium	1968	Raisa Obodovskaya, U.S.S.R.
1962	Beryl Burton, G.B.	1969	Raisa Obodovskaya, U.S.S.R.
1963	Beryl Burton, G.B.		
1964	Yvonne Reynders, Belgium		

1970	Tamara Garkuskina, U.S.S.R.	1975	Keetie Van Oosten-Hage, Neth.
1971	Tamara Garkuskina, U.S.S.R.	1976	Keetie Van Oosten-Hage, Neth.
1972	Tamara Garkuskina, U.S.S.R.	1977	Vera Kuzmetsova, U.S.S.R.
1973	Tamara Garkuskina, U.S.S.R.	1978	Keetie Van Oosten-Hage, Neth.
1974	Tamara Garkuskina, U.S.S.R.		

Road Race

1958	Elsy Jacobs, Luxembourg	1968	Keetie Hage, Neth.
1959	Yvonne Reynders, Belgium	1969	Audrey McElmury, U.S.
1960	Beryl Burton, G.B.	1970	Anna Konkina, U.S.S.R.
1961	Yvonne Reynders, Belgium	1971	Anna Konkina, U.S.S.R.
1962	Marie-Rosa Gaillard, Belgium	1972	Genevieve Gambillon, France
1963	Yvonne Reynders, Belgium	1973	Nicole Van Den Broeck, Belgium
1964	Emmilla Sonk, U.S.S.R.	1974	Genevieve Gambillon, France
1965	Elizabeth Eicholz, E. Germany	1975	Trijnte Fopma, Neth.
1966	Yvonne Reynders, Belgium	1976	Keetie Van Oosten-Hage, Neth.
1967	Beryl Burton, G.B.	1977	Josiane Bost, France
		1978	Beate Jabetz, W. Germany

World Women's Speed Records

Outdoor

Unpaced standing start:

Distance	min.: sec.	
1 km	1:15.1	Irena Kirichenko (U.S.S.R.) at Yerevan, U.S.S.R., Oct. 8, 1966
5 km	6:44.75	Keetie van Oosten-Hage (Neth.) at Munich, W. Germany, Sept. 16, 1978
10 km	13:34.39	Keetie van Oosten-Hage (Neth.) at Munich, W. Germany, Sept. 16, 1978
20 km	27:26.66	Keetie van Oosten-Hage (Neth.) at Munich, W. Germany, Sept. 16, 1978
100 km	2 hr 41:32.6	Maria Cressari (Italy) at Milan, Italy, Oct. 17, 1974
26 miles 1,355 yd	1 hour	Keetie van Oosten-Hage (Neth.) at Munich, W. Germany, Sept. 16, 1978

Unpaced flying start:

Distance	min. : sec.	
200 m	12.3	Lyubov Razuvayeva (U.S.S.R.) at Irkutsk, U.S.S.R., July 17, 1955
500 m	31.7	Galina Tzareva (U.S.S.R.) at Tbilisi, U.S.S.R., Oct. 8, 1978
1,000 m	1:12.9	Lyubov Razuvayeva (U.S.S.R.) at Irkutsk, U.S.S.R., July 17, 1955

Indoor Tracks

Unpaced standing start:

Distance	min. : sec.	
1,000 m	1:15.5	Elizabeth Eicholz (E. Germany) at East Berlin, E. Germany, March 4, 1964

Unpaced flying start:

Distance	min. : sec.	
200 m	13.2	Karla Günther (E. Germany) at East Berlin, E. Germany, March 7, 1964
500 m	35.0	Karla Günther (E. Germany) at East Berlin, E. Germany, March 7, 1964

Equestrian Sports

Evidence of horse-riding dates from a Persian engraving of *c.* 3000 B.C. Pignatelli's academy of horsemanship at Naples dates from the 16th century. The earliest jumping competition was at the Agricultural Hall, London, in 1869. Equestrian events have been included in the Olympic Games since 1912, with women allowed to take part since the 1952 Olympic Games at Stockholm.

World Championship Competition

Women generally compete head-to-head against the men in equestrian competition. There was a women's world championship in show jumping inaugurated in 1965, but the competition was held only three times, and is no longer run as a separate event. The winners of this competition were:

Show Jumping

1965   Marion Coakes, Great Britain, on "Stroller"
1970   Janou Lefebvre, France, on "Rocket"
1974   Janou Lefebvre Tissot, France, on "Rocket"

Dressage

World championships for dressage were instituted in 1966, and are held every four years. They have been won by women in the following years:
1970   Elena Petouchkova (U.S.S.R.) on "Pepel"
1978   Christine Stückelberger (Switzerland) on "Granat"

Three-Day Event

World championships in the three-day event were instituted in 1966, and have been held every four years since. The event has been won by a woman once:
1970   Mary Gordon-Watson, Great Britain
      on "Cornishman V"

Olympic Games

The only one of the three Olympic equestrian events in which a woman has won an individual gold medal is the dressage competition, but women have won medals in jumping and in the three-day event as well.

Dressage—Individual Gold Medalists

1972   Liselott Lisenhoff (W. Germany) on "Piaff"
1976   Christine Stückelberger (Switzerland) on "Granat"

In addition to her 1972 individual gold, Lisenhoff was a member of the West German teams which won the gold medal in 1968 and the silver in 1956 and 1972, and she took the individual bronze medal in 1956.

Christine Stückelberger was a member of the Swiss team which won the silver medal in 1976.

Anne Moore of Great Britain is one of several women who have won Olympic medals outside the dressage event, with her individual silver medal win in jumping at the 1972 Games.

First Solo Transcontinental Journey

Nan Jane Aspinwall left San Francisco, California, on horseback on September 1, 1910. She arrived in New York City on July 8, 1911, having covered 4,500 miles in 301 days, 108 of which she spent traveling.

Fencing

Fencing (fighting with single sticks) was first practiced as a sport in Egypt as early as *c.*1360 B.C. Men's competition includes three weapons, the foil, the epée and the sabre, but women use only the foil, which originally served as the practice weapon for the short court sword in the 17th century, and is the oldest of the three. The women's international championship began at the 1924 Olympic Games at Paris. Individual foil competition has been included on the Olympic program since that time, and in addition, an annual world championship for women in non-Olympic years was inaugurated in 1929. The team championship began in 1932, but was not accepted as an Olympic event until the 1960 Games.

Competition

The foil itself is the same for men's and women's events, and the protective garments worn are similar, except for the additional breast protectors worn inside the jacket by female competitors. The winner in women's fencing is the first competitor to score four hits (versus five in men's competition). The time limit is also slightly shorter, 5 minutes for women as opposed to 6 minutes for men.

World Championship

In Olympic years the competition at the Games is considered the world championship event. Olympic champions are indicated with asterisks in the listings which follow.

Individual Foil

1924* Ellen Osiier, Denmark	1951 Ilona Elek, Hungary
1928* Helene Mayer, Germany	1952* Irene Camber, Italy
1929 Helene Mayer, Germany	1953 Irene Camber, Italy
1930 Jenny Addams, Belgium	1954 Karen Lachmann,
1931 Helene Mayer, Germany	Denmark
1932* Ellen Preis, Austria	1955 Lydia Domolki, Hungary
1933 Gwen Neligan, G.B.	1956* Gillian Sheen, G.B.
1934 Ilona Elek, Hungary	1957 Alexandra Zabelina,
1935 Ilona Elek, Hungary	U.S.S.R.
1936* Ilona Elek, Hungary	1958 Valentina Kisseleva,
1937 Helene Mayer, Germany	U.S.S.R.
1938 Marie Sediva, Czech.	1959 Elena Efimova, U.S.S.R.
1939–46 No competition	1960* Heidi Schmid, Germany
1947 Ellen Preis, Austria	1961 Heidi Schmid, Germany
1948* Ilona Elek, Hungary	1962 Olga Orban Szabo,
1949 Ellen Preis, Austria	Rumania
1950 Renee Garilhe, France, and	1963 Ildiko Uljaki-Retjo,
Ellen Preis, Austria (tie)	Hungary

1964*	Ildiko Uljaki-Retjo, Hungary	1971	Marie Chantal Demaille, France
1965	Galina Gorokhova, U.S.S.R.	1972*	Antonella Ragno-Lonzi, Italy
1966	Tatyana Samusenko, U.S.S.R.	1973	Valentina Nikonova, U.S.S.R.
1967	Alexandra Zabelina, U.S.S.R.	1974	Ildiko Bobis, Hungary
1968*	Elena Novikova Belova, U.S.S.R.	1975	Ecaterina Stahl, Rumania
		1976*	Ildiko Bobis, Hungary
1969	Elena Novikova Belova, U.S.S.R.	1977	Valentina Sidorova, U.S.S.R.
1970	Galina Gorokhova, U.S.S.R.	1978	Valentina Sidorova, U.S.S.R.

Team Foil

1932	Denmark	1953	Hungary	1966	U.S.S.R.
1933	Hungary	1954	Hungary	1967	Hungary
1934	Hungary	1955	Hungary	1968*	U.S.S.R.
1935	Hungary	1956	U.S.S.R.	1969	Rumania
1936	Germany	1957	Italy	1970	U.S.S.R.
1937	Hungary	1958	U.S.S.R.	1971	U.S.S.R.
1938–1946	No competition	1959	Hungary	1972*	U.S.S.R.
1947	Denmark	1960*	U.S.S.R.	1973	Hungary
1948	Denmark	1961	U.S.S.R.	1974	U.S.S.R.
1949	No competition	1962	Hungary	1975	U.S.S.R.
1950	France	1963	U.S.S.R.	1976*	U.S.S.R.
1951	France	1964*	Hungary	1977	U.S.S.R.
1952	Hungary	1965	U.S.S.R.	1978	U.S.S.R.

Most Olympic Medals

The women's record is seven medals by Ildiko Ujlaki-Rejto (later Sagine-Rejto, born in Hungary, May 11, 1937). She won two gold medals (individual and team, 1964), three silver (team, 1960, 68, 72) and two bronze (individual, 1968; team, 1976).

Three women have won the world championship three times —Helene Mayer, Ellen Preis (later Muller-Preis) and Ilona Elek (later Schacherer-Elek). Of the three, only Elek won two individual Olympic titles.

In the Olympic team foil competition, the U.S.S.R. has taken the gold medal four of the five times the event has appeared on

Germany's Helene Mayer has won three women's foil world championships (1929, 31, 37), a record she shares with two others.

the program, and won the silver medal in the only other competition (1964). Elena Novikova Belova of the U.S.S.R. has won three team golds, one individual gold and an individual bronze in the years 1968–1976.

Field Hockey

A representation of two hoop players with curved snagging sticks apparently in an orthodox "bully" position was found in Tomb No. 17 at Beni Hasan, Egypt, and has been dated to c.2050 B.C. There is a British reference to the game in Lincolnshire in 1277. The first country to form a national association was England with the first Hockey Association founded at Cannon Street Hotel, London, in 1875. The first international match pitted Wales against Ireland on January 26, 1895.

The earliest women's field hockey club was East Molesey in Surrey, England, formed in c.1887. The first national association was the Irish Ladies' Hockey Union founded in 1894. The first international match was an England versus Ireland game in Dublin in 1896, which Ireland won, 2–0.

Field hockey was introduced into the U.S. in 1901 by Constance Applebee, a British physical education teacher who demonstrated the game to a group of students at the Harvard

Summer School in Massachusetts. Miss Applebee was persuaded to teach the game to students at a number of women's colleges, including Vassar, Wellesley, Smith, Mount Holyoke and Bryn Mawr, and presided at the meeting in 1922 which gave birth to the United States Field Hockey Association.

In the U.S. field hockey is primarily a game played by girls, particularly on the college and high school level, although this is not the case internationally. Women's field hockey will appear for the first time on the Olympic program for the 1980 Games—men's field hockey has been an Olympic event since 1908.

Highest International Score

The highest score in a women's international match occurred when England defeated France 23–0 at Merton, Greater London, on February 3, 1923.

Highest Attendance

The highest attendance at a women's hockey match was 65,165 for the match between England and the U.S. at the Empire Stadium, Greater London, England, on March 11, 1978.

Fishing

Women's World Fishing Records

The following are records for sea fish taken by tackle as ratified by the International Game Fish Association as of September 1, 1978.

Amberjack, Greater 101 lb. 0 oz.
   by Cynthia Boomhower at Palm Beach, Florida, March 31, 1970
Barracuda 66 lb. 4 oz.
   by Mme. M. Halley at Cape Lopez, Gabon, July 17, 1955

Bass, Giant Sea   452 lb. 0 oz.
  by Lorene Wheeler at Coronado Island, Mexico, October 8, 1960
Cobia   97 lb. 0 oz.
  by Mary W. Black at Oregon Inlet, North Carolina, June 4, 1952
Cod   81 lb. 12 oz.
  by Sophie Karwa at Middlebank, Massachusetts, September 24, 1970
Marlin, Black   1,525 lb. 0 oz.
  by Kimberley Wiss at Cabo Blanco, Peru, April 22, 1954
Marlin, Atlantic Blue   1,018 lb. 8 oz.
  by Linda Koerner at South Pass, Louisiana, July 23, 1977
Marlin, Pacific Blue   674 lb. 0 oz.
  by Charlotte E. Ferreira at Waikiki, Oahu, Hawaii, April 15, 1978
Marlin, Striped   401 lb. 0 oz.
  by Margaret Williams, Cavalli Island, New Zealand, February 24, 1970
Marlin, White   142 lb. 0 oz.
  by Marie Beneventi at Fort Lauderdale, Florida, March 14, 1959
Sailfish, Atlantic   108 lb. 4 oz.
  by Ellen Botha at Luanda, Angola, March 30, 1971
Sailfish, Pacific   199 lb. 0 oz.
  by Carolyn B. Brinkman at Pinas Bay, Panama, January 17, 1968
Shark, Blue   410 lb. 0 oz.
  by Martha C. Webster at Rockport, Massachusetts, August 17, 1967
Shark, Porbeagle   369 lb. 0 oz.
  by Patricia W. Smith at Looe, Cornwall, U.K., July 20, 1970
Shark, Shortfin Mako   911 lb. 12 oz.
  by Audrey Cohen at Palm Beach, Florida, April 9, 1962
Shark, Thresher   729 lb. 0 oz.
  by Mrs. V. Brown at Mayor Island, New Zealand, June 3, 1959
Shark, Tiger   1, 314 lb. 0 oz.
  by Mrs. B. Dyer at Cape Moreton, Queensland, Australia, July 27, 1953
Shark, White   1, 052 lb. 0 oz.
  by Mrs. B. Dyer at Cape Moreton, Queensland, Australia, June 27, 1954
Swordfish   772 lb. 0 oz.
  by Mrs. L. Marron at Iquique, Chile, June 7, 1954
Tarpon   203 lb. 0 oz.
  by June Jordan at Marathon, Florida, May 19, 1961
Tuna, Atlantic Bigeye   332 lb. 14 oz.
  by Waltraud Lehmann at Mogan Port, Canary Islands, June 16, 1977
Tuna, Pacific Bigeye   336 lb. 0 oz.
  by Mrs. S. Knox at Cabo Blanco, Peru, January 16, 1957
Tuna, Bluefin   1,139 lb. 0 oz.
  by Patricia M. Kunle at North Lake, Prince Edward Island, Canada,
    September 26, 1976
Tuna, Yellowfin   261 lb. 8 oz.
  by Evangeline Komo at Kailua, Kona, Hawaii, July 4, 1978
Wahoo   113 lb. 0 oz.
  by Jan K. Bates at Yanuca, Fiji, June 30, 1967

Games and Pastimes

BRIDGE

Bridge (a corruption of Biritch) is thought to be of Levantine origin, similar games having been played there in the early 1870's. The game was known in London in 1886 under the title of "Biritch or Russian Whist."

Most Master Points

In 1971, a new World Ranking List based on Master Points was instituted. The world's leading woman player is Mrs. Rixi Markus of Great Britain, with 269 points to March, 1978.

Two queens of card playing are Mrs. Rixi Markus (left), the reigning women's bridge champion, and Ardeth Hardy (right), who dealt blackjack for a record 169 hours 47 minutes.

CARD PLAYING

Ardeth Hardy, a dealer at the King 8 Casino in Las Vegas, Nevada, spent 169 hours 47 minutes dealing at the blackjack table, starting on June 22, 1977, to set the women's marathon record. She took 5-minute rest breaks within each hour.

Nona Gaprindashvili is the current women's chess champion, a title she has held since 1962.

CHESS

The name chess is derived from the Persian word *shah*. It is a descendant of the game *Chaturanga*. The earliest reference is from the Middle Persian Karnamak (*c.*590–628), though there are grounds for believing its origins are from the 2nd century, owing to the discovery announced in December, 1972, of two ivory chessmen in the Uzbek Soviet Republic, datable to that century. The first women's chess tournament was won by Lady Thomas Hastings of England on August 5, 1895.

World Championship

The women's world championship has been held the longest by Vera Menchik-Stevenson (Great Britain, 1906–44) from 1927 until her death, and was successfully defended a record seven times. Nona Gaprindashvili (U.S.S.R.) has held the title since 1962, and defended four times.

Women's World Champions

1927–44	Vera Menchik-Stevenson (G.B.)
1944–49	No champion recognized
1950	Ludmila Rudenko (U.S.S.R.)
1953	Elizaveta Bykova (U.S.S.R.)
1956	Olga Rubtsova (U.S.S.R.)
1958	Elizaveta Bykova (U.S.S.R.)
1962	Nona Gaprindashvili (U.S.S.R.)

Women's World Team Champions

1957	U.S.S.R.	1972	U.S.S.R.
1963	U.S.S.R.	1974	U.S.S.R.
1966	U.S.S.R.	1976	Israel
1969	U.S.S.R.	1978	U.S.S.R.

These four high school students (clockwise from lower left), Gayle Fields, Marian Selby, Lori Daulton and Charlotte Rugar, hold the marathon chess-playing record.

Marathon

The longest recorded marathon chess-playing session is one of 158 hours 24 minutes by Lori Daulton, Marian Selby, Charlotte Rugar and Gayle Fields (two separate pairs) from Dinwiddie County Junior High School, Dinwiddie, Virginia, December 17–23, 1977.

Gliding

Emanuel Swedenborg of Sweden made sketches of gliders *c.* 1714. The earliest man-carrying glider was designed by Sir George Cayley and carried his coachman about 500 yards across a valley near Brompton Hall, Yorkshire, England, in the summer of 1853. Gliders now attain speeds of 168 m.p.h., and the Jastrzab acrobatic sailplane is designed to withstand vertical dives at up to 280 m.p.h.

Women's World Gliding Records

The following are the international gliding records as of March 1979 for single-seater craft.

Height Gain	9,119 m by Anne Burns (G.B.) in Skylark 3B, January 13, 1961
Absolute Distance	12,557.75 m by Sabrina Jackintell (G.B.) in Astir CS, February 14, 1979
Straight Distance	810 km by Adela Dankowska (Poland) in Jantar 1, April 19, 1977
Goal Flight	731.6 km by Tamara Zaiganova (U.S.S.R.) in A-15, July 29, 1966
Goal and Return	714.7 km by Hanna Reitsch (W. Germany) in Std Cirrus, June 3, 1978
Triangular Distance	779.68 km by Elizabeth Karel (Australia) in LS-3, January 24, 1979
100 km Triangle	139 km/hr by Susan Martin (Australia) in LS-3, February 2, 1979
300 km Triangle	121.54 km/hr by Elizabeth Karel (Australia) in LS-3, January 30, 1979
500 km Triangle	133.14 km/hr by Susan Martin (Australia) in LS-3, January 29, 1979
750 km Triangle	95.4 km/hr by Elizabeth Karel (Australia) in LS-3, January 24, 1979

Golf

Although a stained glass window in Gloucester Cathedral, Scotland, dating from 1350 portrays a golfer-like figure, the earliest mention of golf occurs in a prohibiting law passed by the Scottish Parliament in March, 1457, under which "golff be utterly cryit doune." The Romans had a cognate game called *paganica,* which may have been carried to Britain before 400 A.D. The Chinese National Golf Association claims the game is of Chinese origin from the 3rd or 2nd century B.C. Gutta percha balls succeeded feather balls in 1848, and were in turn succeeded in 1902 by rubber-cored balls, invented in 1899 by Coburn Haskell (U.S.). Steel shafts on clubs were authorized in 1929.

Women began playing golf very early in the game's history. Mary Queen of Scots (1542-87) played during her reign at St. Andrews, Fife, Scotland, and reportedly made an interesting contribution to the game. She had been educated in France, and referred to the young men who chased the golf balls as "cadets," the French word for "students." This was widely adopted and the pronunciation adapted until it became the word "caddy" as we use today.

The first known golf tournament for women was played at the Musselburgh Golf Club in Scotland in a match between the town fishwives on January 9, 1811. The Ladies' Golf Union was formed in England in 1872, and under their authority, Lady Margaret Scott became the first women's golf champion, winning at Royal Lytham on June 13, 1893.

The United States Golf Association was founded in 1894 to supervise golf for men and women, and when the men had their first amateur championship in 1895 at Newport, Rhode Island, the women met at the Meadow Brook Club course in Westbury, Long Island, New York, to determine the women's champion. Thirteen competitors met in November, 1895, and the winner was Mrs. Charles Brown with an 18–hole score of 132.

Patty Berg, a leader in the organization of women's professional golf, won 41 tournaments between 1948 and 1962.

Professional women golfers organized in 1946 to form the Women's Professional Golfers' Association, with Patty Berg as president. They set up the U.S. Women's Open competition in 1946. In 1950, the Ladies Professional Golf Association was founded, again with Berg as president. They continued the annual Open championship until 1953, when the U.S.G.A. took over the sponsorship. The L.P.G.A. began its own annual championship in 1955, and has continued to expand its activities until today there are over three dozen tournaments on the L.P.G.A. schedule with total purses totaling an estimated $3,400,000 in 1978.

U.S.G.A. Women's Amateur Championship

1895 C. Brown at Meadow Brook G.C., Westbury, N.Y.
1896 Beatrix Hoyt at Morris County G.C., Convent, N.J.
1897 Beatrix Hoyt at Essex County Club, Manchester, Mass.
1898 Beatrix Hoyt at Ardsley Club, Ardsley-on-Hudson, N.Y.
1899 Ruth Underhill at Philadelphia C.C., Bala, Pa.
1900 Frances C. Griscom at Shinnecock Hills G.C., N.Y.
1901 Genevieve Hecker at Baltusrol G.C., Short Hills, N.J.
1902 Genevieve Hecker at The Country Club, Brookline, Mass.
1903 Bessie Anthony at Chicago G.C., Wheaton, Ill.
1904 Georgiana Bishop at Merion Cricket Club, Haverford, Pa.
1905 Pauline Mackay at Morris County G.C., Convent, N.J.
1906 Harriot S. Curtis at Brae Burn C.C., West Newton, Mass.

Glenna Collett Vare won the U.S.G.A. Amateur Championship six times, in 1922, 25, 28–30 and 35.

1907   Margaret Curtis at Midlothian C.C., Blue Island, Ill.
1908   Kate C. Harley at Chevy Chase Club, Md.
1909   Dorothy Campbell at Merion Cricket Club, Haverford, Pa.
1910   Dorothy Campbell at Homewood C.C., Flossmoor, Ill.
1911   Margaret Curtis at Baltusrol G.C., Short Hills, N.J.
1912   Margaret Curtis at Essex County Club, Manchester, Mass.
1913   Gladys Ravenscroft at Wilmington C.C., Del.
1914   Kate Harley Jackson at Nassau C.C., Glen Cove, N.Y.
1915   C. H. Vanderbeck at Onwentsia Club, Lake Forest, Ill.
1916   Alexa Stirling at Belmont Springs C.C., Waverly, Mass.
1917–1918   No competition
1919   Alexa Stirling at Shawnee C.C., Shawnee-on-Delaware, Pa.
1920   Alexa Stirling at Mayfield C.C., Cleveland, Ohio
1921   Marion Hollins at Hollywood G.C., Deal, N.J.
1922   Glenna Collett at Greenbrier G.C., White Sulphur Springs, W. Va.
1923   Edith Cummings at Westchester Biltmore G.C., Rye, N.Y.
1924   Dorothy Campbell Hurd at Rhode Island G.C., Nyatt, R.I.
1925   Glenna Collett at St. Louis C.C., Mo.
1926   Helen B. Stetson at Merion Cricket Club, Haverford, Pa.
1927   Miriam Burns Horn at Cherry Valley Club, Garden City, N.Y.
1928   Glenna Collett at Virginia Hot Springs G.&T.C., Hot Springs, Va.
1929   Glenna Collett at Oakland Hills C.C., Birmingham, Mich.
1930   Glenna Collett at Los Angeles C.C., Cal.
1931   Helen Hicks at C.C. of Buffalo, Buffalo, N.Y.
1932   Virginia Van Wie at Salem C.C., Peabody, Mass.
1933   Virginia Van Wie at Exmoor C.C., Highland Park, Ill.
1934   Virginia Van Wie at Whitemarsh C.C., Chestnut Hill, Pa.
1935   Glenna Collett Vare at Interlachen C.C., Minneapolis, Minn.
1936   Pamela Barton (Great Britain) at Canoe Brook C.C., Summit, N.J.
1937   Estelle Lawson Page at Memphis C.C., Tenn.
1938   Patty Berg at Westmoreland C.C., Wilmette, Ill.

Babe Didrikson Zaharias began playing golf in 1935, and by 1940 had begun a string of victories which encompassed every major amateur and professional title for women. She was selected for the L.P.G.A. Hall of Fame in 1951.

1939   Betty Jameson at Wee Burn Club, Noroton, Conn.
1940   Betty Jameson at Del Monte G.&T.C., Cal.
1941   Betty Hicks Newell at The Country Club, Brookline, Mass.
1942–45   No competition
1946   Babe Didrikson Zaharias at Sunset Hills C.C., Tulsa, Okla.
1947   Louise Suggs at Franklin Hills C.C., Franklin, Mich.
1948   Grace Lenczyk at Pebble Beach Course, Del Monte, Cal.
1949   D. G. Porter at Merion G.C., Ardmore, Pa.
1950   Beverly Hanson at Atlanta Athletic Club, Ga.
1951   Dorothy Kirby at Town and C.C., St. Paul, Minn.
1952   Jacqueline Pung at Waverly C.C., Portland, Ore.
1953   Mary Lena Faulk at Rhode Island G.C., Providence, R.I.
1954   Barbara Romack at Allegheny C.C., Sewickley, Pa.
1955   Pat Lesser at Myers Park C.C., Charlotte, N.C.
1956   Marlene Stewart (Canada) at Meridians Hills C.C., Indianapolis, Ind.
1957   JoAnne Gunderson at Sacramento, Cal.
1958   Anne Quast at Danbury, Conn.
1959   Barbara McIntire at Congressional C.C., Washington, D.C.
1960   JoAnne Gunderson at Tulsa C.C., Okla.
1961   Anne Quast Decker at Tacoma G.&C.C., Wash.
1962   JoAnne Gunderson, Rochester C.C., N.Y.
1963   Anne Quast Welts at Taconic G.C., Williamstown, Mass.
1964   Barbara McIntire at Prairie Dune C.C., Hutchinson, Kan.

1965	Jean Ashley at Lakewood C.C., Denver, Colo.		
1966	JoAnne Gunderson Carner at Sewickley Heights G.C., Pa.		
1967	Lou Dill at Annandale G.C., Pasadena, Cal.		
1968	JoAnne Gunderson Carner at Birmingham C.C., Mich.		
1969	Catherine Lacoste (France) at Las Colinas C.C., Irving, Tex.		
1970	Martha Wilkinson at Wee Burn C.C., Darien, Conn.		
1971	Laura Baugh at Atlanta C.C., Ga.		
1972	Anne Budke at St. Louis C.C., Mo.		
1973	Carol Semple at West Orange, N.J.		
1974	Cynthia Hill at Seattle, Wash.		
1975	Beth Daniel at Newton, Mass.		
1976	Donna Horton at Sacramento, Cal.		
1977	Beth Daniel		
1978	Cathy Sherk (Canada)		

U.S. Women's Open Championship

Year	Winner	Score	Course
1946	Patty Berg	5 & 4 (match play)	Spokane C.C. Spokane, Wash.
1947	Betty Jameson	295	Starmount Forest C.C. Greensboro, N.C.
1948	Babe Zaharias	300	Atlantic City C.C. Northfield, N.J.
1949	Louise Suggs	291	Prince Georges C.C. Landover, Md.
1950	Babe Zaharias	291	Rolling Hills C.C. Wichita, Kan.
1951	Betsy Rawls	293	Druid Hills G.C. Atlanta, Ga.
1952	Louise Suggs	284	Bala G.C. Philadelphia, Pa.
1953	Betsy Rawls (won 18-hole playoff)	302–70	C.C. of Rochester Rochester, N.Y.
1954	Babe Zaharias	291	Salem C.C. Peabody, Mass.
1955	Fay Crocker	299	Wichita C.C. Wichita, Kan.
1956	Kathy Cornelius (won 18-hole playoff)	302–75	Northland C.C. Duluth, Minn.

First year in which prize money was offered. Total purse was $6,000; winner's share, $1,500.

1957	Betsy Rawls	299	Winged Foot G.C. Mamaroneck, N.Y.
1958	Mickey Wright	290	Forest Lake C.C. Detroit, Mich.

1959	Mickey Wright	287	Churchill Valley C.C. Pittsburgh, Pa.
1960	Betsy Rawls	292	Worcester C.C. Worcester, Mass.
1961	Mickey Wright	293	Baltusrol G.C. Springfield, N.J.
1962	Murle Lindstrom	301	Dunes G.C. Myrtle Beach, S.C.
1963	Mary Mills	289 (−3)	Kenwood C.C. Cincinnati, Ohio

Prize money had reached total purse of $9,000, with $1,900 for winner's share.

1964	Mickey Wright	290 (−2)−70	San Diego C.C. Chula Vista, Cal.
1965	Carol Mann	290 (+2)	Atlantic City C.C. Northfield, N.J.

Total purse, $17,780; winner's share, $3,800.

1966	Sandra Spuzich	297 (+9)	Hazeltine Nat. G.C. Minneapolis, Minn.
1967	Catherine LaCoste (only amateur to win open)	294 (+10)	Hot Springs G.C. Hot Springs, Va.
1968	Susie Berning	289 (+5)	Moselem Springs G.C. Fleetwood, Pa.
1969	Donna Caponi (Young)	294 (−2)	Scenic Hills C.C. Pensacola, Fla.

Total purse, $25,000; winner's share, $5,000.

1970	Donna Caponi (Young)	287 (−1)	Muskogee C.C. Muskogee, Ok.
1971	JoAnne Carner	288 (even)	Kahkwa C.C. Erie, Pa.
1972	Susie Berning	299 (+11)	Winged Foot G.C. Mamaroneck, N.Y.

Total purse, $40,000; winner's share, $6,000.

1973	Susie Berning	290 (+2)	C.C. of Rochester Rochester N.Y.
1974	Sandra Haynie	295 (+7)	La Grange C.C. La Grange, Ill.
1975	Sandra Palmer	295 (+7)	Atlantic City C.C. Northfield, N.J.

Total purse, $55,000; winner's share, $8,044.

1976	JoAnne Carner (won 18-hole playoff)	292(+8)(−76)	Rolling Green C.C. Springfield, Pa.
1977	Hollis Stacy	292(+4)	Hazeltine Nat. G.C. Chaska, Minn.

Total purse, $75,000; winner's share, $11,040.

1978	Hollis Stacy	289	C.C. of Indianapolis Indianapolis, Ind.

Louise Suggs won 50 professional tournaments in her career, and was the leading money winner on the L.P.G.A. tour in 1953 and 1960.

Betsy Rawls had her best season in 1959, when she won 10 tournaments (including the L.P.G.A. Championship), was awarded the Vare Trophy and took home $27,000, which that year was the highest total for a woman golfer. She now serves as L.P.G.A. Tournament director.

L.P.G.A. Championship

Year	Winner	Score	Course
1955	Beverly Hanson (won 36-hole playoff)	220, 4 & 3	Orchard Ridge C.C. Ft. Wayne, Ind.
1956	Marlene Hagge (won sudden-death playoff)	291	Forest Lake C.C. Detroit, Mich.
1957	Louise Suggs	285	Churchill Valley C.C. Pittsburgh, Pa.

First year in which prize money was offered. Total purse was $7,600; winner's share, $1,500.

1958	Mickey Wright	288	Churchill Valley C.C. Pittsburgh, Pa.
1959	Betsy Rawls	288	Sheraton Hotel C.C. French Lick, Ind.
1960	Mickey Wright	292	Sheraton Hotel C.C. French Lick, Ind.
1961	Mickey Wright	287	Stardust C.C. Las Vegas, Nev.

Total purse, $15,000; winner's share, $2,500.

1962	Judy Kimball	282	Stardust C.C. Las Vegas, Nev.
1963	Mickey Wright	294(+10)	Stardust C.C. Las Vegas, Nev.
1964	Mary Mills	278(−6)	Stardust C.C. Las Vegas, Nev.
1965	Sandra Haynie	279(−5)	Stardust C.C. Las Vegas, Nev.
1966	Gloria Ehret	282(−2)	Stardust C.C. Las Vegas, Nev.
1967	Kathy Whitworth	284(−8)	Pleasant Valley C.C. Sutton, Mass.
1968	Sandra Post (won 18-hole playoff)	294(+2)−68	Pleasant Valley C.C. Sutton, Mass.

Total purse, $20,000; winner's share, $3,000.

| 1969 | Betsy Rawls | 293(+1) | Concord G.C. Kiamesha Lake, N.Y. |

Total purse, $35,000; winner's share, $5,250.

| 1970 | Shirley Englehorn (won sudden-death playoff) | 285(−7) | Pleasant Valley C.C. Sutton, Mass. |
| 1971 | Kathy Whitworth | 288(−4) | Pleasant Valley C.C. Sutton, Mass. |

Total purse, $53,000; winner's share, $7,950.

1972	Kathy Ahern	293(+1)	Pleasant Valley C.C. Sutton, Mass.
1973	Mary Mills	288(−4)	Pleasant Valley C.C. Sutton, Mass.
1974	Sandra Haynie	288(−4)	Pleasant Valley C.C. Sutton, Mass.
1975	Kathy Whitworth	288(−4)	Pine Ridge C.C. Baltimore, Md.
1976	Betty Burfeindt	287(−5)	Pine Ridge C.C. Baltimore, Md.
1977	Chako Higuchi	279(−9)	Bay Tree Plantation N. Myrtle Beach, S.C.

Total purse, $150,000; winner's share, $22,500.

| 1978 | Nancy Lopez | 275 | Jack Nicklaus G.C. Kings Island, Ohio |

Curtis Cup

Of the five international team matches in which the U.S. participates, only the Curtis Cup is a women's event. The biennial competition, first held in 1930, matches 6-member amateur teams from the U.S. (selected by the U.S.G.A.) against the British Isles (selected by the Ladies' Golf Union). The cup was donated by Margaret and Harriot S. Curtis of Boston, each of whom had won the U.S.G.A. Women's Amateur Championship (Margaret in 1907, 11 and 12; Harriot in 1906).

1930	Informal match at Sunningdale, England. Score British Isles 6, U.S. 6
1932	U.S. 5$\frac{1}{2}$, B.I. 3$\frac{1}{2}$, at Wentworth, England
1934	U.S. 6$\frac{1}{2}$, B.I. 2$\frac{1}{2}$, at Chevy Chase, Md.
1936	U.S. 4$\frac{1}{2}$, B.I. 4$\frac{1}{2}$, at Gleneagles, Scotland
	(Note: In case of tie, the defenders retain the cup.)
1938	U.S. 5$\frac{1}{2}$, B.I. 3$\frac{1}{2}$, at Manchester, Mass.
1940–46	No competition
1948	U.S. 6$\frac{1}{2}$, B.I. 2$\frac{1}{2}$, at Southport, England
1950	U.S. 7$\frac{1}{2}$, B.I. 1$\frac{1}{2}$, at Buffalo, N.Y.
1952	B.I. 5, U.S. 4, at Muirfield, Scotland
1954	U.S. 6, B.I. 3, at Ardmore, Pa.
1956	B.I. 5, U.S. 4, at Sandwich, England
1958	B.I. 4$\frac{1}{2}$, U.S. 4$\frac{1}{2}$, at West Newton, Mass. (defenders retain cup)
1960	U.S. 6$\frac{1}{2}$, B.I. 2$\frac{1}{2}$, at Lindrick, Nottinghamshire, England
1962	U.S. 8, B.I. 1, at Colorado Springs, Colo.
1964	U.S. 10$\frac{1}{2}$, B.I. 7$\frac{1}{2}$, at Wales, U.K.
1966	U.S. 13, B.I. 5, at Hot Springs, Va.
1968	U.S. 10$\frac{1}{2}$, G.B. 7$\frac{1}{2}$, at Newcastle, Northern Ireland
1970	U.S. 11$\frac{1}{2}$, G.B. 6$\frac{1}{2}$, at West Newton, Mass.
1972	U.S. 10, G.B. 8, at Western Gailes, Scotland
1974	U.S. 13, G.B. 5, at San Francisco, Cal.
1976	U.S. 11$\frac{1}{2}$, G.B. 6$\frac{1}{2}$, at Lytham, England
1978	U.S. 12, G.B. 6, at Apawamis, N.Y.

Lowest Scores*

72 Holes

The lowest recorded L.P.G.A. tournament score for 72 holes is 271 by Hollis Stacy at the Rail Golf Club, Springfield, Illinois, in the 1977 Rail Muscular Dystrophy Classic. Her total consisted of rounds of 68–65–69–69, finishing up 17 under par.

* L.P.G.A. records except as noted

54 Holes

Two golfers have carded 200 strokes for 54 holes in L.P.G.A. competition, Ruth Jessen (69–65–64) at the Omaha J.C. Open in 1964, and Carol Mann (66–66–68) at the Canongate Country Club in Palmetto, Georgia, in 1968 to win the Lady Carling Open.

36 Holes

The L.P.G.A. low score over 36 holes is 131, first shot in the 1976 Birmingham Classic in Alabama by Kathy Martin at Green Valley Country Club (66–65), and equalled in the 1977 Lady Keystone Open at Armitage Country Club, Harrisburg, Pennsylvania by Silvia Bertolaccini (66–65).

18 Holes

The lowest recorded score on an 18-hole course (over 6,000 yards) for a woman is 62 (30 + 32) by Mickey Wright at Hogan Park Golf Club, Midland, Texas, in the final round of the 1964 Tall City Open. In a non-L.P.G.A. competition held over a shorter course (5,002 yards), Wanda Morgan recorded a score of 60 (31 + 29) on the Westgate-on-Sea and Birchington Golf Club course on July 11, 1929.

Carol Mann (left) shot 54 holes in 200 strokes to tie the L.P.G.A. record in 1968. Mickey Wright (right) holds the 18-hole scoring record along with the record for tournament wins, with 82 professional victories.

Kathy Whitworth had won a record $813,213 by the end of the 1978 season.

9 Holes

There have been three 29-stroke scores for nine holes reported in L.P.G.A. competition. Marlene Hagge shot a 29 at the Raymond Memorial Golf Course at Columbus, Ohio, in 1971. Carol Mann shot a 7-under-par 29 on the first nine holes of the first round in the 1975 Borden Classic, and went on to complete the round in 66. Most recently, Pat Bradley shot a 29 on the back nine of the third round of the 1978 Golden Lights Championship. Her nine-hole score was 7 under par, and her total for the round was 64.

Most Tournament Wins

Mickey Wright won 82 professional tournaments up to June, 1978. She is one of two golfers to have won the U.S. Women's Open four times (1958, 59, 61, 64), the other being Betsy Rawls (1951, 53, 57, 60). Wright's record also includes four L.P.G.A. championships (1958, 60, 61, 63), making her the only woman to hold both the Open and the L.P.G.A. titles in the same year, a feat she has accomplished twice.

The record for most professional tournaments won in a single year is also held by Mickey Wright, with 13 victories in 1963, out of 30 tournaments entered.

Highest Earnings

The record for highest career earnings by a woman is $813,213 by Kathy Whitworth through the end of 1978. Her

In 1978, Nancy Lopez became the first woman to be named both Rookie-of-the-Year and Player-of-the-Year in the same season.

79 tournament wins is second only to Mickey Wright's mark, although in all of these victories she has never been able to win the Open. She does, however, have three L.P.G.A. Championships to her credit.

Nancy Lopez (born January 6, 1957, in Torrance, California) earned $189,814 in 1978, the record for women's golf earnings in a single year. This record is all the more impressive since Ms. Lopez only joined the L.P.G.A. tour in 1977, and her earnings in her rookie year amounted to $30,178 (officially only $23,138, since her second-place money in the Open was not credited to her official standing, as she had not yet become a member of the L.P.G.A.). By 1978 she was not only a full-fledged member but a world record holder and winner of the 1978 L.P.G.A. championship as well.

Holes-in-One

Longest

The longest straight hole ever achieved in one shot is the first hole of the Furnace Brook Golf Club, Wollaston, Massachusetts, a distance of 393 yards, made by Marie Robie on September 4, 1949.

Consecutive

There have been at least 15 cases of aces being achieved in two consecutive holes, one of which was accomplished by a woman, Sue Press, on the 13th and 14th holes at Chatswood Golf Club, Sydney, Australia, on May 29, 1977.

Two in One Round

Two holes-in-one made in one round has been reported on three occasions. Mrs. W. Driver aced the 3rd and 8th holes at Balgowlah Club, New South Wales, Australia, on May 19, 1942. Mrs. F. Burke made holes-in-one on the 2nd and 8th holes of the same club on July 29, 1948. At the Lomas Athletic Club in Argentina, Marjorie Merchant reportedly aced the 4th and 8th holes, but the date is not known.

Consecutive Rounds

In three consecutive rounds (on three separate days) over Easter in 1960, Mrs A. E. "Paddy" Martin scored holes-in-one on the 125-yard 3rd hole of the Rickmansworth Course in England. She used the same ball and the same club (No. 8) each time.

Oldest and Youngest

The oldest woman golfer reported to have made a hole-in-one is Mrs. Lily Parry, who was 81 years 11 months old when she aced the 8th hole of the Pontypridd Golf Course in Wales, U.K. on October 9, 1971.

Two nine-year-old girls have claimed the distinction of being the youngest woman golfer to be credited with a hole-in-one. Mary Venker aced the 128-yard 12th hole at Bloomington, Indiana, on August 13, 1971, and Susan Thompson duplicated this feat on the 115-yard 9th hole at River View, California, on July 19, 1973.

Most Shots for One Hole

A woman player in the qualifying round of the Shawnee Invitational for Ladies at Shawnee-on-Delaware, Pennsylvania, in c.1912, took 166 strokes for the short 130-yard 16th hole. Her tee shot went into the Binniekill River and the ball floated. She put out in a boat with her exemplary, but statistically-minded, husband at the oars. She eventually beached the ball $1\frac{1}{2}$ miles downstream, but was not yet out of the woods. She had to play through a forest on the homeward journey.

Gymnastics

A primitive form of gymnastics was practiced in ancient Greece during the period of the ancient Olympic Games (776 B.C. to 393 A.D.), but the modern sport developed from c.1780. During the 19th century in Europe gymnastic societies were founded which stressed the benefits of gymnastic exercises for men and women, young and old. International competition is supervised by the Federation Internationale de Gymnastique (F.I.G.), which sanctioned the first international women's gymnastic championship in 1950, and continues to set the rules for the F.I.G. World Championships (held every four years) and the Olympic gymnastic competition, which began for women in 1952.

Competition

International competition for women takes place in four events, the horse vault, the uneven bars, the balance beam and floor exercises, with additional titles awarded for combined exercises and team performance.

Horse Vault: The horse is the same as the men's horse except that it is placed sideways to the competitor (as opposed to the men's lengthwise approach) and is set 1.10 meters off the floor (1.35 meters for men).

Uneven Bars: As opposed to the men's parallel bar competition, where the two bars are set at the same height, the women's apparatus is set with the top bar 2.40 meters from the floor, the lower bar 1.50 meters from the floor. The distance between the bars varies depending on the competitor's height.

Balance Beam: The beam is 10 centimeters wide, 5 meters long and raised above the ground 120 centimeters. The exercise must include exhibitions of balance, large and small turns, jumps and leaps, running steps, and some held or posed positions.

Floor Exercises: The floor exercise is generally similar to the men's event, performed on a 12-meter-square mat. The women's exercises, though, are performed to music, and run from 60-90 seconds.

World Championships

In Olympic years the competition at the Games is considered the world championship event. Olympic champions are indicated with asterisks in the listings which follow.

Combined Exercises

1950   Helena Rakoczy (Poland)
1952* Maria Gorokhovskaya (U.S.S.R.)
1954   Galina Roudiko (U.S.S.R.)
1956* Larissa Latynina (U.S.S.R.)
1958   Larissa Latynina (U.S.S.R.)
1960* Larissa Latynina (U.S.S.R.)
1962   Larissa Latynina (U.S.S.R.)

1964* Vera Caslavska (Czech.)
1966   Vera Caslavska (Czech.)
1968* Vera Caslavska (Czech.)
1970   Ludmilla Tourischeva (U.S.S.R.)
1972* Ludmilla Tourischeva (U.S.S.R.)
1974   Ludmilla Tourischeva (U.S.S.R.)
1976* Nadia Comaneci (Rumania)
1978   Elena Mukhina (U.S.S.R.)

Uneven Bars

1950   Trude Kolar (Austria) and Anna Petterson (Sweden)
1952* Margit Korondi (Hungary)
1954   Agnes Keleti (Hungary)
1956* Agnes Keleti (Hungary)
1958   Larissa Latynina (U.S.S.R.)
1960* Polina Astakhova (U.S.S.R.)
1962   Irina Pervushina (U.S.S.R.)
1964* Polina Astakhova (U.S.S.R.)
1966   Natalia Kuchinskaya (U.S.S.R.)
1968* Vera Caslavska (Czech.)
1970   Karin Janz (East Germany)

Karin Janz won 2 gold medals, 1 silver and 1 bronze at the 1972 Olympics.

1972* Karin Janz (East
     Germany)
1974 Annelore Zinke (East
     Germany)

1976* Nadia Comaneci
      (Rumania)
1978 Marcia Frederick (U.S.)

Balance Beam

1950 Helena Rakoczy (Poland)
1952* Nina Bocharova (U.S.S.R.)
1954 Keiko Tanaka (Japan)
1956* Agnes Keleti (Hungary)
1958 Larissa Latynina
     (U.S.S.R.)
1960* Eva Bosakova (Czech.)
1962 Eva Bosakova (Czech.)
1964* Vera Caslavska (Czech.)
1966 Natalia Kuchinskaya
     (U.S.S.R.)

1968* Natalia Kuchinskaya
      (U.S.S.R.)
1970 Erika Zuchold (East
     Germany)
1972* Olga Korbut (U.S.S.R.)
1974 Ludmilla Tourischeva
     (U.S.S.R.)
1976* Nadia Comaneci
      (Rumania)
1978 Nadia Comaneci
     (Rumania)

Horse Vault

1950 Helena Rakoczy (Poland)
1952* Yekaterina Kalinchuk
     (U.S.S.R.)
1954 Anna Petterson (Sweden)
     and Tamara Manina
     (U.S.S.R.)
1956* Larissa Latynina
     (U.S.S.R.)
1958 Larissa Latynina
     (U.S.S.R.)
1960* Margarita Nikolayeva
     (U.S.S.R.)

1962 Vera Caslavska (Czech.)
1964* Vera Caslavska (Czech.)
1966 Vera Caslavska (Czech.)
1968* Vera Caslavska (Czech.)
1970 Erika Zuchold (East
     Germany)
1972* Karin Janz (East
     Germany)
1974 Olga Korbut (U.S.S.R.)
1976* Nelli Kim (U.S.S.R.)
1978 Nelli Kim (U.S.S.R.)

Floor Exercises

1950 Helena Rakoczy (Poland)
1952* Agnes Keleti (Hungary)
1954 Tamara Manina
     (U.S.S.R.)
1956* Agnes Keleti (Hungary)
     and Larissa Latynina
     (U.S.S.R.)
1958 Eva Bosakova (Czech.)
1960* Larissa Latynina
     (U.S.S.R.)
1962 Larissa Latynina
     (U.S.S.R.)
1964* Larissa Latynina (U.S.S.R.)

1966 Natalia Kuchinskaya
     (U.S.S.R.)
1968* Larissa Petrik (U.S.S.R.)
     and Vera Caslavska
     (Czech.)
1970 Ludmilla Tourischeva
     (U.S.S.R.)
1972* Olga Korbut (U.S.S.R.)
1974 Ludmilla Tourischeva
     (U.S.S.R.)
1976* Nelli Kim (U.S.S.R.)
1978 Nelli Kim (U.S.S.R.)

Olga Korbut won the hearts of millions of spectators at the 1972 Olympic Games, along with her 4 medals, 3 gold and a silver. By the 1976 Games, she was out of the limelight but still a winning competitor, with a gold and a silver medal. She has since retired from competition.

Team

1950	Sweden	1966	Czechoslovakia
1952*	U.S.S.R.	1968*	U.S.S.R.
1954	U.S.S.R.	1970	U.S.S.R.
1956*	U.S.S.R.	1972*	U.S.S.R.
1958	U.S.S.R.	1974	U.S.S.R.
1960*	U.S.S.R.	1976*	U.S.S.R.
1962	U.S.S.R.	1978	U.S.S.R.
1964*	U.S.S.R.		

In the 1928, 1936 and 1948 Olympic Games there was a team title only for women gymnasts. The winners were Netherlands, 1928; Germany, 1936; Czechoslovakia, 1948.

Most World Championship Titles

The women's record for both individual and total world championship titles is held by Larissa Semyonovna Latynina (born December 27, 1934; retired 1966) of the U.S.S.R., who won ten individual championships and five team titles between 1956 and 1964.

Larissa Latynina won 9 Olympic gold medals and 15 world championship titles.

Most Olympic Medals

The greatest number of individual gold medals in Olympic competition by a woman in any event is seven, by gymnast Vera Caslavska-Odlozil (born in Czechoslovakia, May 3, 1942). She won three in 1964 and four (one shared) in 1968.

Larissa Latynina won six individual gold medals and was a member of three gold medal teams, for a total of nine gold medals. She also won five silver and four bronze Olympic medals, making 18 in all—an Olympic record for either sex in any sport.

Highest Olympic Score

The first perfect score in Olympic gymnastics, a 10.0, went to Nadia Comaneci (born in Rumania, November 12, 1961) for her first appearance on the uneven bars at the 1976 Olympics. She followed this up with another six perfect 10.0 scores, three more on the uneven bars and three on the balance beam, winning a total of three individual gold medals, a silver medal in the team event and an individual bronze medal.

Nelli Kim (born in U.S.S.R., July 29, 1957) was awarded two perfect scores as well at the 1976 Games. She took home four medals, two individual gold, one team gold, and a silver.

Nadia Comaneci displays her perfect form on the balance beam at the 1976 Olympic Games, where she won a total of five medals.

World Cup

The first World Cup gymnastic competition was held in London in 1975. Ludmilla Tourischeva (born in U.S.S.R., October 7, 1952) won all five gold medals available. Her stock

The leading gymnasts at the 1976 Olympics were (left to right) Ludmilla Tourischeva, Nelli Kim and Nadia Comaneci, seen here accepting their medals for the floor exercise competition.

of Olympic medals consists of 3 golds (team in 1972 and 1976, individual combined exercises 1972), 3 silvers (floor exercises 1972 and 1976, horse vault 1976) and a bronze in the horse vault in 1972.

Largest Crowd

The largest recorded crowd for a gymnastics competition was approximately 18,000 who packed the Forum at Montreal, Canada, for the finals of the women's individual apparatus competitions at the XXI Olympic Games on July 22, 1976. Comparable audiences are reported for the Shanghai Stadium, People's Republic of China.

National Championship

The A.A.U. sponsored the first national women's gymnastic championship in 1931. The organization supervises competition in accordance with F.I.G. rules in Junior and Senior divisions for men and women. In the past the A.A.U. gymnastics competitions included several events which were not on the F.I.G. program, but these have been phased out. They were flying rings (1933–57), tumbling (1938–68), Indian clubs (1941–51), rebound tumbling (1961–68) and trampolining (1962–68). Trampolining and tumbling became a separate competition, not affiliated with the gymnastic events.

All-Around Champions

1931	Roberta C. Ranck	1944	Helm McKee
1932	No competition	1945	Clara Schroth
1933	Consetta Caruccio	1946	Clara Schroth
1934	Consetta Caruccio	1947	Helen Schifano
1935	Thera Steppich	1948	Helen Schifano
1936	Jennie Caputo	1949	Clara M. Schroth
1937	Pearl Perkins	1950	Clara M. Schroth
1938	Helm McKee	1951	Clara M. Schroth
1939	Margaret Weissmann	1952	Clara Schroth Lomady
1940	No competition	1953	Ruth Grulkowski
1941	Pearl Perkins Nightingale	1954	Ruth Grulkowski
1942	No competition	1955	Ernestine Russell
1943	Pearl Perkins Nightingale	1956	Sandra Ruddick

1957	Muriel Davis	1968	Linda Metheny
1958	Ernestine Russell	1969	Joyce Tanac
1959	Ernestine Russell	1970	Linda Metheny
1960	Gail Sontgerath	1971	Linda Metheny
1961	Kazuki Kadowaki	1972	Linda Metheny
1962	Dale McClements	1973	Joan Moore Rice
1963	Muriel Grossfeld	1974	Joan Moore Rice
1964	Marie Walther	1975	Ann Carr
1965	Doris Fuchs Brause	1976	Roxanne Pierce
1966	Linda Metheny	1977	Stephanie Willim
1967	Carolyn Hacker		

Most A.A.U. Titles

Clara Schroth (later Mrs. Lomady) is unbeaten in the number of national championship titles she won in each of the individual events and the all-around championship. She won the floor exercise competition seven times (1944–46, 48, 50–52), the horse vault six times (1944, 45 (tied), 48, 49, 51, 52), the balance beam ten times (1941, 43–51), and along with Doris Fuchs, won the uneven bars competition four times (1946, 49, 50, 52).

Chinning the Bar

The women's record for one-handed chin-ups is 27 in Hermann's Gym, Philadelphia, in 1918, by Lillian Leitzel (Mrs. Alfredo Codona) (U.S., 1892–1931). Her total would be unmatched by any male, but it is doubtful if they were achieved from a "dead hang" position.

Leitzel achieved her remarkable strength as a world-famous circus performer. Born Leopoldina Alitza Pelikan, she was a star of the Ringling Brothers Barnum and Bailey Circus by 1919. The 4-foot-9-inch, 95-lb. aerial gymnast would perform intricate maneuvers on rings suspended 50 feet above the ground. The most spectacular part of her act was a rapid series of one-arm planges, in which she grasped the rope with one hand and twisted her body up and around, rotating like a propeller, over and over again as the band played "Flight of the Bumblebee" and the crowd counted her turns in unison. She did 100 of these one-arm planges at every performance (although in later years she tapered off to 60), and once reached a total of 239 without stopping—and always without a net!

An extraordinary athlete and performer, Lillian Leitzel was a featured act with the Ringling Brothers Barnum and Bailey Circus.

As she was performing on the rings at the Valencia Music Hall in Copenhagen, Denmark, on February 13, 1931, the equipment broke and she plummeted 29 feet to the floor below. She died two days later.

Vertical Jump

The greatest height by a woman in a vertical jump, that is, the difference between the height of the fingertip reach while standing and in jumping, is 30 inches by Olympic pentathlon champion Mary Peters (Great Britain, born July 6, 1939) in California in 1972.

Mary Peters set a new women's vertical jump record in 1972, the year she won the Olympic pentathlon.

Handball (Field)

This internationally popular game is played by teams of 12 on a marked indoor court with a ball approximately 7 inches in diameter, and should not be confused with the game of court handball or 4-wall handball which is more frequently played in the U.S. Handball was first played c.1895. International competition began in 1935, and by 1977 there were some 70 countries affiliated with the International Handball Federation (founded 1946).

Competition

No more than seven team members may be in play at one time. The game resembles soccer in many ways, except that the rest of the body is used instead of the feet. Players can run three steps with the ball before either passing or bouncing the ball, and points are scored by sending the ball between the posts and under the crossbar of a soccer-style goal.

Women play two 25-minute halves (men play 30-minute halves); otherwise the rules for both sexes are similar.

Olympic Competition

Handball was introduced into the Olympic Games at Berlin in 1936 as an 11-a-side outdoor game, then was dropped from the program and was not reinstated until 1972, when the 7-a-side men's event was introduced. The first women's Olympic handball competition took place in 1976 at Montreal, where the U.S.S.R. won the gold medal, East Germany won the silver medal and Hungary won the bronze. The members of the Soviet team were the following:

Natalia Sherstjuk   Tatyana Glustchenko
Rafiga Shabanova   Ludmila Shubina
Lubov Berezhnaya   Galina Zakharova
Zinaida Turchina   Aldona Chesaitite
Tatyana Makarets   Nina Lobova
Maria Litoshenko   Ludmila Pantchuk
Ludmila Bobrus   Larisa Karlova

World Championship Titles

The most victories won in World Championship competition (instituted 1938) are by Rumania, with three women's titles between 1956 and 1974.

Harness Racing

The trotting gait (the simultaneous use of the diagonally opposite legs) was first recorded in England in c.1750. The sulky first appeared in harness racing in 1829.

Most Successful Woman Driver

The top woman harness driver in North America, and probably in the world, has been Bea Farber of Brighton, Michigan (born November 8, 1940). She won the first International Women's Driving Tournament, sponsored by the U.S. Trotting Association in the fall of 1978. Representatives from eight different countries competed at five different American harness tracks in a total of 16 races. Farber won the tournament with 367 points, beating her nearest rival, Agnese Palagi of Italy, by 121. She has won similar contests in Europe in the last three years.

Farber is a lifetime winner of just under 25 per cent of her drives. She won her very first race, at a county fair in Bay City, Michigan, and her second parimutuel start, at Jackson, Michi-

Bea Farber has driven more than 3,000 races, including 92 wins out of 333 starts in the 1978 season.

gan on May 1, 1971. She was the first woman ever to go in 2 minutes over a half-mile track, driving "Easy Irv" at Jackson Raceway. In 1978, her best season to date, she became the first woman driver to make harness racing's Top Ten list in the major category (300 drives or more in a year). She finished second in the national rankings with her .432 UDRS. Her winnings totaled $1,465,427 through the 1978 season.

Horse Racing

Horsemanship was an important part of the Hittite culture of Anatolia, Turkey, dating from 1400 B.C. The 33rd ancient Olympic Games in 648 B.C. featured horse racing. The earliest horse race recorded in England was one held in about 210 A.D. at Netherby, North Yorkshire, among Arabians brought to Britain by Lucius Septimus Severus, Emperor of Rome. Horse racing in the United States began somewhat later, with the first recorded race taking place in c.1665 at Hempstead, New York. The first jockey club in the world was the original Charleston Jockey Club in Virginia, which was organized in 1734.

First Women Jockeys

It is difficult to pin down precisely the identity of the first woman to ride in a race, given the long association of women and horses and the human predilection, when mounted side by side on horses, to race them. It is known that Alicia Meynell rode against Captain William Flint over a 4-mile course at York, England, on August 25, 1804, and was present again at the York August Meeting of 1805, at which time she won two races. She was, it might be noted, the mistress of the horse's owner. Eileen Joel had similar assistance in procuring a mount, in her status as daughter of a millionaire. She won in a 4-mile race, the Newmarket Town Plate, in Newmarket, England, against 8 competitors, 5 of whom were women.

On a more professional level there is English-born Judy Johnson, who participated in a steeplechase event at Pimlico Racetrack, Baltimore, Maryland, on April 27, 1943. She finished tenth out of eleven entries aboard "Lone Gallant."

In 1968 and 1969 there was a concerted effort on the part of several women to secure the honor of riding as the first licensed female jockey. This was not an easy task, though, since they all met with substantial resistance from established jockeys. Penny Ann Early, for instance, was granted a license by the Kentucky State Racing Commission in November, 1968, with the proviso that she race twice before the end of the season. She had three opportunities to fill this requirement, but the first time the track was muddy and her horse was scratched. The second time she found a male jockey had been given her mount on the morning of the race, and on her last eligible day, the male jockeys boycotted the race. Barbara Jo Rubin also faced a boycott by male jockeys, each of whom was fined $100 for his refusal to race.

Kathy Kusner became the first licensed jockey in the U.S. in 1968, although the first woman jockey to appear at a pari-mutuel racetrack was Diane Crump, on February 7, 1969. The first winning woman jockey was Barbara Jo Rubin, who rode "Cohesian" to win by a neck at Charles Town, West Virginia on February 22, 1969. Rubin won the first race by a woman at a major track as well, riding "Bravy Galaxy," a first-time starter, to victory at Aqueduct Racetrack in New York.

The first woman to win a major stakes race, and by most accounts the most successful woman on the racing scene today,

Robyn Smith has been a formidable competitor at major New York race tracks since her first stakes victory in 1973.

is Robyn Smyth. Her stakes victory came on March 1, 1973, when she won the $27,450 Paumanauk Handicap aboard "North Sea" at Aqueduct. She began her racing career in California in 1969, and had her first mount at Aqueduct the same year.

Women raced against each other under Jockey Club rules in England in May, 1972, in the Goya Stales at Kempton Park. The winner was ridden by Meriel Tufnell. The first woman in Europe to ride against professional jockeys was Anna-Marie la Ponche of France, in March, 1974.

Ice Skating

The earliest reference to ice skating is in early Scandinavian literature referring to the 2nd century, though its origins are believed, on archeological evidence, to be ten centuries earlier still. The earliest English account, from 1180, refers to skates made of bone. The earliest known illustration is a Dutch woodcut from 1498. The first iron-bladed skates were made in 1572.

Figure Skating

Two Americans were instrumental in the development of figure skating as an art. The first, E. W. Bushnell of Philadelphia, invented steel blades for skates in 1850. His discovery became popular immediately, and provided the precision skate needed for figure-skating maneuvers. The man who brought art to figure skating was Jackson Haines, a ballet master who transferred the movements of the dance to the ice while in Vienna in 1864, and continued to innovate, teach and demonstrate until his death in 1875.

One of Haines' pupils, Louis Rubinstein, helped to found the Amateur Skating Association of Canada in 1878, the first of the skating organizations throughout the world. In 1879 the National Skating Association of Great Britain was founded, in 1887 the Skating Club of the United States was organized, and by 1892, the Internationale Eislauf-Vereinigung (International Skating Union) was founded in the Netherlands. This organization continues to govern international competition.

Women's World Championship

Individual

1906	Madge Syers, Great Britain	1925	Herma Planck Szabo, Austria
1907	Madge Syers, Great Britain	1926	Herma Planck Szabo, Austria
1908	Lily Kronberger, Hungary	1927	Sonja Henie, Norway
1909	Lily Kronberger, Hungary	1928	Sonja Henie, Norway
1910	Lily Kronberger, Hungary	1929	Sonja Henie, Norway
1911	Lily Kronberger, Hungary	1930	Sonja Henie, Norway
1912	Meray Horvath, Hungary	1931	Sonja Henie, Norway
1913	Meray Horvath, Hungary	1932	Sonja Henie, Norway
1914	Meray Horvath, Hungary	1933	Sonja Henie, Norway
1915–21	No competition	1934	Sonja Henie, Norway
1922	Herma Planck Szabo, Austria	1935	Sonja Henie, Norway
1923	Herma Planck Szabo, Austria	1936	Sonja Henie, Norway
1924	Herma Planck Szabo, Austria	1937	Cecilia Colledge, Great Britain
		1938	Megan Taylor, Great Britain

1939	Megan Taylor, Great Britain
1940–46	No competition
1947	Barbara Ann Scott, Canada
1948	Barbara Ann Scott, Canada
1949	Alena Vrzanova, Czechoslovakia
1950	Alena Vrzanova, Czechoslovakia
1951	Jeanette Altwegg, Great Britain
1952	Jacqueline du Bief, France
1953	Tenley Albright, U.S.
1954	Gundi Busch, Germany
1955	Tenley Albright, U.S.
1956	Carol Heiss, U.S.
1957	Carol Heiss, U.S.
1958	Carol Heiss, U.S.
1959	Carol Heiss, U.S.
1960	Carol Heiss, U.S.
1961	No competition
1962	Sjoukje Dijkstra, Netherlands
1963	Sjoukje Dijkstra, Netherlands
1964	Sjoukje Dijkstra, Netherlands
1965	Petra Burka, Canada
1966	Peggy Fleming, U.S.
1967	Peggy Fleming, U.S.
1968	Peggy Fleming, U.S.
1969	Gabriele Seyfert, E. Germany
1970	Gabriele Seyfert, E. Germany
1971	Beatrix Schuba, Austria
1972	Beatrix Schuba, Austria
1973	Karen Magnussen, Canada
1974	Christine Errath, E. Germany
1975	Dianne de Leeuw, Netherlands
1976	Dorothy Hamill, U.S.
1977	Linda Fratianne, U.S.
1978	Annett Poetzsch, E. Germany

In 1976, Dorothy Hamill won the world championship, the Olympic gold medal and the U.S. national championship.

Most World Championship Titles

Individual

The women's record for individual titles is 10 (equal to Ulrich Salchow's record for men) by Sonja Henie (born Oslo,

Sonja Henie parlayed her ice skating expertise into a huge personal fortune through ice shows and motion picture performances.

Norway, April 8, 1912, died October 12, 1969). Her incredible record of figure skating titles began when she was only 10 years old with the figure skating championship of Norway. Along with her world championship titles, she won the gold medal at three consecutive Olympic Games (1928–36) in the individual competition. She also held the European title a total of 8 times, and the Norwegian title 6 times.

After the 1936 Olympics, Henie turned professional, promoting her own touring ice shows and starring in 11 films, including such self-explanatory titles as *Thin Ice, Iceland, Wintertime* and *Happy Landing*. In the process she built up the popularity of figure skating in the United States, along with her personal fortune. For many years she held the record for greatest earnings by a sporting figure, male or female, with an estimated $47,500,000. It took the mighty Muhammad Ali to defeat her in this category.

Pairs

Irina Rodnina (born U.S.S.R., September 12, 1949) has won ten world championship titles in the pairs competition (instituted 1908). She won four times with Aleksiy Ulanov (born November 4, 1947), from 1969 through 1972, and six with her husband Aleksandr Zaitsev (born June 16, 1952), from 1973 through 1978.

Irina Rodnina has won a total of 10 world pairs titles, six of them with her husband Aleksandr Zaitsev (shown here).

Ice Dancing

The ice dance competition was instituted in 1950, when the American pair, Lois Waring and Michael McGean, won the title. The greatest number of wins is six by Ludmila Pakhomova (born December 31, 1946) and Aleksandr Gorshkov (born December 8, 1946), who won in 1970–74 and 1976.

Ludmila Pakhomova and Aleksandr Gorshkov have dominated ice dance competition, winning six world championships and the first gold medal awarded in Olympic competition, in 1976.

Olympic Games

Individual Gold Medalists

1908	Madge Syers, G.B.	1948	Barbara Scott, Canada
1920	Magda Julin-Mauroy, Sweden	1952	Jeanette Altwegg, G.B.
1924	Herma Planck-Szabo, Austria	1956	Tenley Albright, U.S.
1928	Sonja Henie, Norway	1960	Carol Heiss, U.S.
1932	Sonja Henie, Norway	1964	Sjoukje Dijkstra, Neth.
1936	Sonja Henie, Norway	1968	Peggy Fleming, U.S.
		1972	Beatrix Schuba, Austria
		1976	Dorothy Hamill, U.S.

Pairs Gold Medalists

1908 Anna Hubler and Heinrich Burger, Germany
1920 Ludovika Jakobsson and Walter Jakobsson, Finland
1924 Helene Engelmann and Alfred Berger, Austria
1928 Andree Joly and Pierre Brunet, France
1932 Andree Brunet and Pierre Brunet, France
1936 Maxi Herber and Ernst Baier, Germany
1948 Micheline Lannoy and Pierre Baugniet, Belgium
1952 Ria Falk and Paul Falk, Germany
1956 Elisabeth Schwarz and Kurt Oppelt, Austria
1960 Barbara Wagner and Robert Paul, Canada
1964 Ludmilla Belousova and Oleg Protopopov, U.S.S.R.
1968 Ludmilla Belousova and Oleg Protopopov, U.S.S.R.
1972 Irina Rodnina and Alexei Ulanov, U.S.S.R.
1976 Irina Rodnina and Aleksandr Zaitsev, U.S.S.R.

Ice Dance Gold Medalists

1976 Ludmila Pakhomova and Aleksandr Gorshkov, U.S.S.R.

"Triple Crown"

The only woman to twice win the "Grand Slam" of World, Olympic and European figure skating titles in the same year was Sonja Henie, in the years 1932 and 1936. Only one man has ever accomplished this double feat, Karl Schäfer of Austria, in the same two years.

Highest Marks

The highest number of maximum six marks awarded for one performance in an international championship was 11 to Irina

Rodnina and Aleksandr Zaitsev (U.S.S.R.) in the European pairs competition in Zagreb, Yugoslavia, in 1974.

Most Difficult Jump

A quadruple twist lift has been performed by only one pair, Marina Tcherkasova (born 1962) and Sergei Shakrai (born 1957) of the U.S.S.R., in an international competition at Helsinki, Finland, on January 26, 1977. They were also the first skaters to accomplish simultaneous triple jumps in international competition at Strasbourg, France, on February 1, 1978.

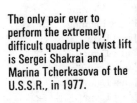

The only pair ever to perform the extremely difficult quadruple twist lift is Sergei Shakrai and Marina Tcherkasova of the U.S.S.R., in 1977.

U.S. National Championship

The U.S. figure skating championship for women and men began in 1914, primarily through the efforts of Irving Brokaw of New York, who popularized the European style of figure skating in America. Held in New Haven, Connecticut, the first competition was won by Theresa Weld of Massachusetts in the singles division. The tournament was an on-again off-again proposition until the formation of the United States Figure Skating Association in 1921.

Individual

1914	Theresa Weld	1948	Gretchen Merrill
1915–17	No competition	1949	Yvonne Sherman
1918	Mrs. R. S. Beresford	1950	Yvonne Sherman
1919	No competition	1951	Sonya Klopfer
1920	Theresa Weld	1952	Tenley Albright
1921	Theresa Weld Blanchard	1953	Tenley Albright
1922	Theresa Weld Blanchard	1954	Tenley Albright
1923	Theresa Weld Blanchard	1955	Tenley Albright
1924	Theresa Weld Blanchard	1956	Tenley Albright
1925	Beatrix Loughran	1957	Carol Heiss
1926	Beatrix Loughran	1958	Carol Heiss
1927	Beatrix Loughran	1959	Carol Heiss
1928	Maribel Y. Vinson	1960	Carol Heiss
1929	Maribel Y. Vinson	1961	Laurence Owen
1930	Maribel Y. Vinson	1962	Barbara Roles Pursley
1931	Maribel Y. Vinson	1963	Lorraine Hanlon
1932	Maribel Y. Vinson	1964	Peggy Fleming
1933	Maribel Y. Vinson	1965	Peggy Fleming
1934	Suzanne Davis	1966	Peggy Fleming
1935	Maribel Y. Vinson	1967	Peggy Fleming
1936	Maribel Y. Vinson	1968	Peggy Fleming
1937	Maribel Y. Vinson	1969	Janet Lynn
1938	Joan Tozzer	1970	Janet Lynn
1939	Joan Tozzer	1971	Janet Lynn
1940	Joan Tozzer	1972	Janet Lynn
1941	Jane Vaughn	1973	Janet Lynn
1942	Jane Vaughn Sullivan	1974	Dorothy Hamill
1943	Gretchen Merrill	1975	Dorothy Hamill
1944	Gretchen Merrill	1976	Dorothy Hamill
1945	Gretchen Merrill	1977	Linda Fratianne
1946	Gretchen Merrill	1978	Linda Fratianne
1947	Gretchen Merrill		

Pairs

Theresa Weld Blanchard and Nathaniel W. Niles won the pairs competition (instituted 1914) a record nine times, in 1918, 20–27.

Ice Dancing

The ice dance championship, instituted in 1960, has been won most often by Judy Schwomeyer and James Sladky, who took five consecutive titles, 1968–72.

Speed Skating

There seems little doubt that there has been speed-skating racing by men and women for almost as long as there has been skating. It is known that women's races took place in the Netherlands as early as 1805. The first world championship races for women were held in 1936, and in 1960 women's speed skating became an Olympic event, with competition held at four different distances. There had been three demonstration events for women speed skaters at the 1932 Winter Olympics at Lake Placid, New York.

Women's World Champions, All-Around

1936	Kit Klein, U.S.
1937	Laila Schou-Nilsen, Norway
1938	Laila Schou-Nilsen, Norway
1939	Verne Lesche, Finland
1940–46	No competition
1947	Verne Lesche, Finland
1948	Maria Isakova, U.S.S.R.
1949	Maria Isakova, U.S.S.R.
1950	Maria Isakova, U.S.S.R.
1951	Eva Huttunen, Finland
1952	Lidia Selikhova, U.S.S.R.
1953	Khalida Schegoleyeva, U.S.S.R.

Tatyana Averina holds two Olympic records for speed skating and won the all-around championship in 1978.

1954	Lidia Selikhova, U.S.S.R.
1955	Rimma Zhukova, U.S.S.R.
1956	Zofia Kondakova, U.S.S.R.
1957	Inga Artamonova, U.S.S.R.
1958	Inga Artamonova, U.S.S.R.
1959	Tamara Rylova, U.S.S.R.
1960	Valentina Stenina, U.S.S.R.
1961	Valentina Stenina, U.S.S.R.
1962	Inga Artamonova Voronina, U.S.S.R.
1963	Lydia Skoblikova, U.S.S.R.
1964	Lydia Skoblikova, U.S.S.R.
1965	Inga Artamonova Voronina, U.S.S.R.
1966	Valentina Stenina, U.S.S.R.
1967	Stien Kaiser, Neth.
1968	Stien Kaiser, Neth.
1969	Lasma Kauniste, U.S.S.R.
1970	Atje Keulen-Deelstra, Neth.
1971	Nina Statkevich, U.S.S.R.
1972	Atje Keulen-Deelstra, Neth.

1973	Atje Keulen-Deelstra, Neth.	1975	Karin Kessow, E. Germany
1974	Atje Keulen-Deelstra, Neth.	1976	Sylvia Burka, Canada
		1977	Vera Bryndzey, U.S.S.R.
		1978	Tatyana Averina, U.S.S.R.

Olympic Games

Women's Speed Skating, Gold Medalists

500 Meters

1960	Helga Haase, Germany	1972	Anne Henning, U.S.
1964	Lydia Skoblikova, U.S.S.R.	1976	Sheila Young, U.S.
1968	Ludmila Titova, U.S.S.R.		

Olympic Record: 42.76 seconds by Sheila Young, 1976

1,000 Meters

1960	Klala Guseva, U.S.S.R.	1972	Monika Pflug, W. Germany
1964	Lydia Skoblikova, U.S.S.R.	1976	Tatyana Averina, U.S.S.R.
1968	Carolina Geijssen, Neth.		

Olympic Record: 1 minute 28.43 seconds by Tatyana Averina, 1976

1,500 Meters

1960	Lydia Skoblikova, U.S.S.R.	1972	Dianne Holum, U.S.
1964	Lydia Skoblikova, U.S.S.R.	1976	Galina Stepanskaya, U.S.S.R.
1968	Kaija Mustonen, Finland		

Olympic record: 2 minutes 16.58 seconds by Galina Stepanskaya, 1976

3,000 Meters

1960	Lydia Skoblikova, U.S.S.R.	1972	Stein Baas-Kaiser, Neth.
1964	Lydia Skoblikova, U.S.S.R.	1976	Tatyana Averina, U.S.S.R.
1968	Johanna Schut, Neth.		

Olympic record: 4 minutes 45.19 seconds by Tatyana Averina, 1976

Lydia Skoblikova has won more gold medals in speed skating than anyone else, with two in 1960 and a sweep of all four distances in 1964.

Women's World Speed Skating Records*

Distance	min:sec	
500 meters	40.68	Sheila Young (U.S.) at Inzell, W. Germany, March 13, 1976
1,000 meters	1:23.46	Tatyana Averina (U.S.S.R.) at Medeo, U.S.S.R., March 29, 1975
1,500 meters	2:07.18	Khalida Vorobyeva (U.S.S.R.) at Medeo, U.S.S.R., April 10, 1978
3,000 meters	4:31.00	Galina Stepanskaya (U.S.S.R.) at Medeo, U.S.S.R., March 23, 1976

*Ratified by the I.S.U. as of June 1, 1978.

The fastest woman on skates is Sheila Young, who has been clocked at over 27 m.p.h. She also won distinction as world cycling champion in 1973 and 1976.

Fastest Speed Skater

Sheila Young (born Detroit, Michigan, October 14, 1950) averaged a speed of 27.49 m.p.h. when she set the women's 500 meter record on March 13, 1976. She has also achieved distinction as a bicyclist, winning the world championship in the sprint competition in 1973 and 1976.

Lugeing

In lugeing the rider adopts a sitting, as opposed to a prone, position on the sled. Official international competition began at Klosters, Switzerland, in 1881. The first European championships were at Reichenberg, E. Germany, in 1914, and the first world championships at Oslo, Norway, in 1955, with women's championships instituted two years later in Austria. Lugeing became an Olympic sport in 1964.

Women's World Championships

1955	K. Kienzl, Austria
1957	M. Isser, Austria
1958	M. Semczyszak, Poland
1959	E. Lieber, Austria
1960	M. Isser, Austria
1961	E. Naegele, Switzerland
1962	Ilse Geisler, E. Germany
1963	Ilse Geisler, E. Germany
1964*	Ortrun Enderlein, E. Germany
1965	Ortrun Enderlein, E. Germany
1966	Ortrun Enderlein, E. Germany
1967	Ortrun Enderlein, E. Germany
1968*	Erica Lechner, Italy
1969	P. Tierlich, W. Germany
1970	Barbara Piecha, Poland
1971	Elisabeth Demleitner, W. Germany
1972*	Anna-Maria Muller, E. Germany
1973	Margit Schumann, E. Germany
1974	Margit Schumann, E. Germany
1975	Margit Schumann, E. Germany
1976*	Margit Schumann, E. Germany
1977	Margit Schumann, E. Germany
1978	Vera Sosulya, U.S.S.R.

Mountaineering

Although bronze-age artifacts have been found on the summit of the Riffelhorn in Switzerland (9,605 feet), mountaineering as a sport has a continuous history dating back only to 1854.

Three women have reached the top of Mount Everest, the most recent being Wanda Rutkiewicz of Poland, in October, 1978.

Mount Everest

To date, three women have reached the peak of Mount Everest, the 29,028-foot summit first reached on May 29, 1953 by Edmund Percival Hillary and the Sherpa, Tenzing Norgay. The first woman to reach the top was Junko Tabei of Japan (born 1940) who reached the summit on May 17, 1975, after a month of climbing. There were fifteen women on the expedition, but an avalanche injured ten, and only Tabei and a male Sherpa reached the top.

Shortly thereafter, on May 27, 1975, the second woman reached the summit. Mrs. Phantog of Tibet was a member of a party of nine who successfully scaled Everest.

The most recent success by a woman was on October 16, 1978, when Wanda Rutkiewicz of Poland arrived at the summit along with Siegfried Hupfauer and Wilhelm Klimek (W. Germany), Robert Allenbach (Switzerland) and three Sherpas.

Olympic Games

At the instigation of Pierre de Fredi, Baron de Coubertin, the Olympic Games of the modern era were inaugurated in Athens on April 6, 1896. Women first participated in tennis and golf in 1900, although these competitions appear to have been incidental to the Games, and were quickly dropped from the program. More formal Olympic competition for women began in 1912 with the inclusion of women's swimming events. The first Winter Olympic competitions were the ice skating events held in conjunction with the 1908 Games in London, and women were included from the beginning, with Madge Syers of Great Britain winning the first individual figure skating title.

Enriqueta Basilio carried the Olympic torch and lit the Olympic flame at the 1968 Games at Mexico City, the first woman to receive this honor.

Number of Women Competitors

The following charts indicate the total number of women competitors at each of the Summer and Winter Games to date, excluding demonstration sports.

Summer Games

Year	No.	Year	No.	Year	No.	Year	No.
1896	0	1912	57	1936	328	1964	683
1900	11	1920	64	1948	385	1968	781
1904	8	1924	136	1952	518	1972	1,070
1906	7	1928	290	1956	384	1976	1,274
1908	36	1932	127	1960	610		

Winter Games

Year	No.	Year	No.	Year	No.	Year	No.
1908	7	1932	32	1956	132	1972	217
1920	12	1936	80	1960	144	1976	276
1924	13	1948	77	1964	200		
1928	27	1952	109	1968	228		

Orienteering

Orienteering was invented by Major Ernst Killander in Sweden in 1918. World championships were inaugurated in 1966 and are held biennially under the auspices of the International Orienteering Federation (founded 1961), located in Sweden. The U.S. Orienteering Federation was founded in 1971 to serve as governing body for the sport in America and choose teams for world championship competition.

Women's World Championships

Individual

1966	Ulla Lindquist, Sweden
1968	Ulla Lindquist, Sweden
1970	Ingrid Hadler, Norway
1972	Sarolta Monspart, Finland
1974	Mona Norgaard, Denmark
1976	Liisa Veijalainen, Finland
1978	Ann Berit Eid, Norway

Team

1966	Sweden
1968	Norway
1970	Sweden
1972	Finland
1974	Sweden
1976	Sweden
1978	Finland

Parachute Jumping

Parachuting graduated from pure life-saving, through stunt exhibitions to a regulated sport with the institution of world championships at Lesce-Bled, Yugoslavia in 1951.

Greatest Accuracy

Jacqueline Smith (Great Britain) scored an unprecented ten consecutive "dead centers" in the world championships at Zagreb, Yugoslavia, August 28–September 1, 1978.

Jacqueline Smith landed a new world record in winning the world championship for parachute jumping accuracy in 1978.

Women's World Championships

Overall

1951	Monique Laroche, France	1970	Marie-France Baulez, France
1954	Valentina Seliverstova, U.S.S.R.	1972	Barbara Karkoschka, E. Germany
1956	Jozka Maxova, Czech.	1974	Natalia Sergeyeva, U.S.S.R.
1958	Nadia Priahina, U.S.S.R.		
1960	Bozena Rejzlova, Czech.	1976	Valentina Zakoreckaja, U.S.S.R.
1962	Muriel Simbro, U.S.		
1964	Tee Taylor, U.S.	1978	Cheryl Stearns, U.S.
1966	L. Jeremina, U.S.S.R.		
1968	Tatyana Voinova, U.S.S.R.		

Accuracy

1962	Dagmar Kuldova, Czech.	1970	Zdena Zarybnicka, Czech.
1964	Valentina Seliverstova, U.S.S.R.	1972	A. Dioujova, U.S.S.R.
		1974	Natalia Mamaj, U.S.S.R.
1966	L. Jeremina, U.S.S.R.	1976	Maria Leadbetter, U.S.
1968	Helena Tomsikova, Czech.	1978	Jacqueline Smith, G.B.

Style

1962	Maria Stancikova, Czech.	1972	Marie-France Baulez, France
1964	Tee Taylor, U.S.		
1966	Tatyana Voinova, U.S.S.R.	1974	Maja Kostjna, U.S.S.R.
1968	Tatyana Voinova, U.S.S.R.	1976	Irin Klabuhn, E. Germany
		1978	Cheryl Stearns, U.S.
1970	Valentina Zakoreckaja, U.S.S.R.		

Team Accuracy

1962	U.S.	1972	Bulgaria
1964	E. Germany	1974	E. Germany
1966	U.S.S.R.	1976	U.S.
1968	Czech.	1978	U.S.
1970	France		

Team Overall

1964	U.S.	1972	U.S.S.R.
1966	U.S.S.R.	1974	U.S.S.R.
1968	U.S.S.R.	1976	U.S.
1970	Czech.	1978	U.S.S.R.

Rodeo

Rodeo came into being with the early days of the North American cattle industry. The earliest references to the sport are from Santa Fe, New Mexico, in 1847. The Girls Rodeo Association was founded in 1948 in Texas, primarily to establish rules for barrel racing, which remains the prime area of rodeo competition for women. The event is a simple race against time in which the rider must gallop around three barrels without tipping them over. The event is increasingly included on the program of rodeos sanctioned by the Professional Rodeo Cowboys Association. In addition, the G.R.A. sponsors All Girl Rodeos throughout the U.S., 25 of which were held in 1978.

G.R.A. Champion Barrel Racers, 1971-1978

1971 Donna Paterson, Tecumseh, Okla.
1972 Gail Petska, Tecumseh, Okla.
1973 Gail Petska, Tecumseh, Okla.
1974 Jeana Day Felts, Woodward, Okla.
1975 Jimmie Gibbs, Valley Mills, Texas
1976 Jimmie Gibbs, Valley Mills, Texas
1977 Connie Combs, Comanche, Okla.
1978 Carol Goostree, Verden, Okla.

Carol Goostree and her horse "Dobre" won $29,647 in barrel races in 1978.

Roller Skating

The first roller skate was devised by Joseph Merlin of Huy, Belgium, in 1760, and first worn by him in public in London. Despite "improved" versions, a really satisfactory roller skate did not materialize until James L. Plimpton of New York produced the present four-wheeled type and patented it in January 1863. The first public rink in the world opened in 1857 in London, England. The great boom periods for roller skating were 1870–75, 1908–12 and 1948–54, each originating in the United States.

Women World Championship —Figure Roller Skating

1947	Ursula Wehrli, Switzerland	1967	Astrid Bader, W. Germany
1949	Franca Rio, Italy	1968	Astrid Bader, W. Germany
1951	Franca Rio, Italy	1970	Christine Kreutzfeldt, W. Germany
1952	Lotte Cadenbach, W. Germany	1971	Petra Hausler, W. Germany
1955	Helene Kienzle, W. Germany	1972	Petra Hausler, W. Germany
1956	Rita Blumenberg, W. Germany	1973	Sigrid Mullenbach, W. Germany
1958	Marika Kilius, W. Germany	1974	Sigrid Mullenbach, W. Germany
1959	Ute Kitz, W. Germany	1975	Sigrid Mullenbach, W. Germany
1961	Marlies Fahse, W. Germany	1976	Natalie Dunn, U.S.
1962	Franzi Schmidt, Switzerland	1977	Natalie Dunn, U.S.
1965	Astrid Bader, W. Germany	1978	Natalie Dunn, U.S.
1966	Astrid Bader, W. Germany		

Fastest Skater

Marisa Danesi attained an average speed of 23.89 m.p.h. when setting the 500 meter record at Inzell, W. Germany, on

September 28, 1968. She also holds the record for greatest distance skated in an hour on a rink, with 21.995 miles, also at Inzell, W. Germany, on September 28, 1968.

Women's World Speed Records

Distance	min : sec	
500 meters	46.8	Marisa Danesi, Italy, at Inzell, W. Germany, September 28, 1968
1,500 meters	2 :18.3	Marisa Danesi, Italy, at Inzell, W. Germany, September 28, 1968
5,000 meters	8 :20.3	Marisa Danesi, Italy, at Inzell, W. Germany, September 28, 1968
100 kilometers	4 hr 38 :51.7	Marretti Carucci, Italy, at Rome, Italy, April 16, 1950

Rowing

The earliest established sculling race is the Doggett's Coat and Badge, which was rowed on August 1, 1716, over five miles from London Bridge to Chelsea, and is still being rowed every year over the same course, under the administration of the Fishmongers' Company. Women's world championship competition was instituted in 1974, with the first Olympic participation in 1976 at Montreal. Women row over a 1,000 meter course, rather than the 2,000 meters rowed by the men.

World Championships

Single Sculls   *Asterisk indicates Olympic title*

1974 Christine Scheiblich, E. Germany

1975 Christine Scheiblich, E. Germany

1976* Christine Scheiblich, E. Germany

1977 Christine Scheiblich, E. Germany

1978 Christine Scheiblich Hahn, E. Germany

Double Sculls

1974 U.S.S.R.
1975 U.S.S.R.
1976* Bulgaria
1977 E. Germany
1978 Bulgaria

Coxless Pairs

1974 Rumania
1975 E. Germany
1976* Bulgaria
1977 E. Germany
1978 E. Germany

Quadruple Sculls

1974 E. Germany
1975 E. Germany
1976* E. Germany
1977 E. Germany
1978 Bulgaria

Coxed Fours

1974 E. Germany
1975 E. Germany
1976* E. Germany
1977 E. Germany
1978 E. Germany

Eights

1974 E. Germany
1975 E. Germany
1976* E. Germany
1977 E. Germany
1978 E. Germany

Women's World Records —1,000 meter course

Event	min:sec	
Single Sculls	3:34.31	Christine Scheiblich, E. Germany, at Amsterdam, Netherlands, August 21, 1977
Double Sculls	3:09.29	E. German pair at Prague, Czech., September 10, 1978
Coxless Pairs	3:26.32	E. German team at Amsterdam, Netherlands, August 21, 1977
Quadruple Sculls	3:03.29	E. German team at Prague, Czech., September 10, 1978
Coxed Fours	3:20.59	E. German team at Amsterdam, Netherlands, August 21, 1977
Eights	2:59.20	U.S.S.R. team at Hamilton, New Zealand, November 1, 1978

Fastest Rower

Christine Scheiblich (now Mrs. Hahn) of East Germany averaged 10.43 m.p.h. when setting the women's record over 1,000 meters of 3 minutes 34.31 seconds at Amsterdam on August 21, 1977.

Shooting

Olympic

The highest placing ever achieved by a woman in Olympic shooting competition is the silver medal by Margaret Murdock of the U.S. (born in Topeka, Kansas, August 25, 1942) in the Small Bore Rifle—3 Position event at Montreal on July 21, 1976. In fact, she had the same score as the winner.

Women's World Records

The following are the official women's world records as of January, 1978.

Standard Rifle at 50 meters, 60 shots prone

Individual—598 by E. Rolinska, Poland, at Suhl, Germany, 1971
          598 by Margaret Murdock, U.S. at Thun, Switzerland, 1974
Team—1780 by Poland at Suhl, Germany, 1971

Standard Rifle, 3 × 20 shots

Individual—582 by Marlies Kanthak, E. Germany at Rome, 1977
Team—1727 by E. Germany at Rome, 1977

Air Rifle at 10 meters, 40 shots

Individual—391 by B. Zarina, U.S.S.R. at Enschede, Netherlands, 1974
Team—1150 by U.S.S.R. at Thun, Switzerland, 1974

Small-Bore Pistol at 25 meters (Center-Fire Program) 60 shots

Individual—592 by Galina Korsun, U.S.S.R. at Rome, 1977
Team—U.S.S.R. at Vingsted, 1974

Air Pistol at 10 meters, 40 shots

Individual—387 by N. Stolijarova, U.S.S.R. at Enschede, Netherlands, 1974

Team—1147 by U.S.S.R. at Enschede, Netherlands, 1974

Trap, 200 birds (Teams: 150)

Individual—195 by Susan Nattrass, Canada, at Seoul, Korea, 1978

Team—395 by Italy at Antibes, 1977

Skeet, 200 birds (Teams: 150)

Individual—189 by Ruth Jordan, W. Germany at Antibes, 1977

Team—410 by W. Germany at Antibes, 1977

Trick Shooting

The most renowned trick shooter of all time was Phoebe Anne Oakley Mozee (Annie Oakley) (1860–1926). She demonstrated the ability to shoot 100 × 100 in trap shooting for 35 years, between the ages of 27 and 62. At 30 paces she could split a playing card end-on, hit a dime in mid-air or shoot a cigarette from the lips of her husband—the courageous Frank Butler.

Annie Oakley took her sharpshooting abilities on the road, performing for many years in traveling Wild West shows.

Skiing

The most ancient ski in existence was found well preserved in a peat bog at Hoting, Sweden, dating from *c*.2500 B.C. A rock carving of a skier at Rodoy, northern Norway, dates from 2000 B.C. Skiing did not develop into a sport, however, until 1843 at Tromso, Norway, and was not introduced into the Alps until 1883. The earliest formal downhill race was staged at Montana, Switzerland, in 1911. The first slalom event was run at Murren, Switzerland, on January 21, 1922. The Winter Olympics were inaugurated on January 25, 1924, and the present governing body for the sport, the International Ski Federation (F.I.S.) was founded on February 2, 1924.

World Championships

The world Alpine championships for both men and women were inaugurated at Murren, Switzerland in 1931. The greatest number of titles won by either sex is 12 by Christel Cranz (born

Christel Cranz of Germany won a record 12 Alpine skiing championships in the years 1934–1939.

Galina Koulakova is seen here winning the 1972 Olympic 10 kilometer event. She holds a total of seven Olympic medals.

July 1, 1914) of Germany. She easily outdistances her nearest male rival, Anton Sailer of Austria, who holds seven titles. Cranz is also a gold medalist in the Olympics, with the Combined event in the 1936 Games.

The greatest number of titles by a woman in the Nordic events is nine by Galina Koulakova of the U.S.S.R. (born April 29, 1942). The male record is eight by Sixten Jernberg of Sweden. Koulakova also holds seven Olympic medals, including four golds (see below), a silver in the 5 kilometer cross-country in 1968 and bronze medals in the 4 × 5 kilometer relay (1968) and the 10 kilometer cross-country (1976).

Women's World Championships —Alpine Skiing

Downhill

Asterisk indicates Olympic title

1931	Esme MacKinnon, Great Britain	1938	Lisa Resch, Germany
1932	Paula Wiesinger, Italy	1939	Christel Cranz, Germany
1933	Inge Wersin-Lantschner, Austria	1948*	Hedy Schlunegger, Switzerland
1934	Anny Rüegg, Switzerland	1950	Trude Jochum-Beiser, Austria
1935	Christel Cranz, Germany	1952*	Trude Jochum-Beiser, Austria
1936	Evelyn Pinching, G.B.		
1937	Christel Cranz, Germany	1954	Ida Schöpfer, Austria

1956* Madeleine Berthod,
       Switzerland
1958 Lucille Wheeler, Canada
1960* Heidi Biebl, W. Germany
1962 Christl Haas, Austria
1964* Christl Haas, Austria
1966 Erika Schinegger, Austria
1968* Olga Pall, Austria

1970 Anneroesli Zyrd,
       Switzerland
1972* Marie-Therese Nadig,
       Switzerland
1974 Annemarie Pröll, Austria
1976* Rosi Mittermaier,
       W. Germany
1978 Annemarie Pröll, Austria

Slalom

1931 Esme MacKinnon,
       Great Britain
1932 Rosli Streiff, Switzerland
1933 Inge Wersin-Lantschner,
       Austria
1934 Christel Cranz, Germany
1935 Anny Rüegg, Switzerland
1936 Gerda Paumgarten,
       Austria
1937 Christel Cranz, Germany
1938 Christel Cranz, Germany
1939 Christel Cranz, Germany

1948* Gretchen Fraser, U.S.
1950 Dagmar Rom, Austria
1952 Andrea Mead-Lawrence,
       U.S.
1954 Trude Klecker, Austria
1956* Renee Colliard,
       Switzerland
1958 Inger Björnbakken,
       Norway
1960* Anne Heggtveit, Canada
1962 Marianne Jahn, Austria

At the 1976 Olympics, Rosi Mittermaier won gold medals in two of the Alpine
skiing events and a silver in the third.

Gretchen Fraser won the women's Olympic slalom race the first time it was contested, in 1948 at St. Moritz.

1964* Christine Goitschel, France	1972* Barbara Cochran, U.S.
1966 Annie Famose, France	1974 Hanny Wenzel, Liechtenstein
1968* Marielle Goitschel, France	1976* Rosi Mittermaier, W. Germany
1970 Ingrid Lafforgue, France	1978 Lea Sölkner, Austria

Combined

1932 Rosli Streiff, Switzerland	1958 Frieda Danzer, Switzerland
1933 Inge Wersin-Lantschner, Austria	1960 Anne Heggtveit, Canada
1934 Christel Cranz, Germany	1962 Marielle Goitschel, France
1935 Christel Cranz, Germany	1964 Marielle Goitschel, France
1936 Evelyn Pinching, Great Britain	1966 Marielle Goitschel, France
1937 Christel Cranz, Germany	
1938 Christel Cranz, Germany	1968 Nancy Greene, Canada
1939 Christel Cranz, Germany	1970 Michelle Jacot, France
1948 Trude Jochum-Beiser, Austria	1972 Annemarie Pröll, Austria
	1974 Fabienne Serrat, France
1954 Ida Schöpfer, Austria	1976 Rosi Mittermaier, W. Germany
1956 Madeleine Berthod, Switzerland	1978 Annemarie Pröll, Austria

Giant Slalom

1950	Dagmar Rom, Austria	1966	Marielle Goitschel, France
1952*	Andrea Mead-Lawrence, U.S.	1968*	Nancy Greene, Canada
1954	Lucienne Schmith-Coultet, France	1970	Betsy Clifford, Canada
1956*	Ossi Reichert, Germany	1972*	Marie-Therese Nadig, Switzerland
1958	Lucille Wheeler, Canada	1974	Fabienne Serrat, France
1960*	Yvonne Rüegg, Switzerland	1976*	Kathy Kreiner, Canada
1962	Marianne Jahn, Austria	1978	Maria Epple, W. Germany
1964*	Marielle Goitschel, France		

World Cup

Introduced in 1967, World Cup competition consists of nine meets, including downhill, slalom and giant slalom events, with the skiers competing for points in each event and the holder of the greatest overall total declared the winner.

1967	Nancy Greene, Canada	1974	Annemarie Pröll, Austria
1968	Nancy Greene, Canada	1975	Annemarie Pröll, Austria
1969	Gertrud Gabl, Austria	1976	Rosi Mittermaier, W. Germany
1970	Michelle Jacot, France		
1971	Annemarie Pröll, Austria	1977	Lise-Marie Morerod,
1972	Annemarie Pröll, Austria	1978	Hanny Wenzel, Liechtenstein
1973	Annemarie Pröll, Austria		

Most Wins, World Cup

Annemarie Pröll (later Mrs. Moser) completed a record sequence of 11 consecutive downhill wins in 1973. In ten seasons, 1970–79, she has won a total of 59 individual events.

Fastest Woman on Skis

The greatest speed attained on skis by a woman is 103.046 m.p.h. by Cathy Breyton, France, at Portillo, Chile, in November 1978.

World Cup champion Annemarie Pröl won consecutive titles in 1971–75.

Women's World Championships —Nordic Skiing

5 Kilometer Cross-Country

Asterisk indicates Olympic title

1962 Alevtina Kolchina, U.S.S.R.
1964* Klaudia Boyarskikh, U.S.S.R.
1966 Alevtina Kolchina, U.S.S.R.
1968* Toini Gustafsson, Sweden
1970 Galina Koulakova, U.S.S.R.

1972* Galina Koulakova, U.S.S.R.
1974 Galina Koulakova, U.S.S.R.
1976* Helena Takalo, Finland
1978 Helena Takalo, Finland

10 Kilometer Cross-Country

1952* Lydia Wideman, Finland
1954 Lyubov Kosyryeva, U.S.S.R.

1956* Lyubov Kosyryeva, U.S.S.R.

1958 Alevtina Kolchina,
      U.S.S.R.
1960* Maria Gusakova, U.S.S.R.
1962 Alevtina Kolchina,
      U.S.S.R.
1964* Klaudia Boyarskikh,
      U.S.S.R.
1966 Klaudia Boyarskikh,
      U.S.S.R.
1968* Toini Gustafsson, Sweden
1970 Alevtina Olyanina,
      U.S.S.R.
1972* Galina Koulakova,
      U.S.S.R.
1974 Galina Koulakova,
      U.S.S.R.
1976* Raisa Smetanina, U.S.S.R.
1978 Zinaida Amosova,
      U.S.S.R.

Klaudia Boyarskikh was the first woman to win 3 Olympic gold medals for skiing.

20 Kilometer Cross-Country

1978 Zinaida Amosova,
      U.S.S.R.

4 × 5 Kilometer Relay (run over 3 stages before 1976)

1954 U.S.S.R.	1968* Norway
1956* Finland	1970 U.S.S.R.
1958 U.S.S.R.	1972* U.S.S.R.
1960* Sweden	1974 U.S.S.R.
1962 U.S.S.R.	1976* U.S.S.R.
1964* U.S.S.R.	1978 Finland
1966 U.S.S.R.	

Longest Ski Jump

The longest ski jump ever recorded by a woman is 321 feet 6 inches by Anita Wold (Norway, born September 21, 1956) at Okura, Sapporo, Japan, on January 14, 1975.

Ski-Bob Championships

Two women have succeeded in retaining the women's world championship title for two successive competitions, Gerhilde Schiffkorn (Austria) in 1967 and 1969, and Gertrude Geberth (Austria) in 1971 and 1973.

Softball

Softball, as an indoor derivative of baseball, was invented by George Hancock at the Farragut Boat Club of Chicago, in 1887. Rules were first codified in Minneapolis in 1895 as Kitten Ball. The game developed as an outdoor sport with dozens of different sets of playing rules, under such names as Mush Ball, Diamond Ball, Playground Ball, Pumpkin Ball, Big Ball, Twilight Ball, Army Ball and Lightning Ball. In 1926 the name Softball came into widespread usage, but it was not until 1933, with the founding of the Amateur Softball Association of America, that international rules were officially adopted and World Series were begun for men and for women. The first of these national championships was held in Chicago in 1933, in conjunction with the World's Fair. This was a fast pitch tournament, as was most of the softball activity until the early 1960's, when the slow pitch version of the game began to gain popularity. Today there are national championships for both fast and slow pitch (slow pitch requires a minimum of a 3-foot arch in the trajectory of the pitch), though the slow pitch game predominates.

The International Softball Federation was formed in 1952 as the governing body for international competition, and now includes 44 countries. There have been four World Championship fast pitch competitions for women to date, the most recent one held in Japan, July 21–30, 1978. Softball has also been included on the schedule for the 1979 Pan-American Games in Puerto Rico.

National Women's Major Fast Pitch Champions ("World Series")

Year	Champions	Tournament Location
1933	Great Northerns, Chicago, Ill.	Chicago, Ill.
1934	Hart Motors, Chicago, Ill.	Chicago, Ill.

1935	Bloomer Girls, Cleveland, Ohio	Chicago, Ill.
1936	National Manufacturing Co., Cleveland, Ohio	Chicago, Ill.
1937	National Manufacturing Co., Cleveland, Ohio	Chicago, Ill.
1938	J. J. Kreig's, Alameda, Cal.	Chicago, Ill.
1939	J. J. Kreig's. Alameda, Cal.	Chicago, Ill.
1940	Arizona Ramblers, Phoenix, Ariz.	Detroit, Mich.
1941	Higgins "Midgets," Tulsa, Okla.	Detroit, Mich.
1942	Jax Maids, New Orleans, La.	Detroit, Mich.
1943	Jax Maids, New Orleans, La.	Detroit, Mich.
1944	Lind & Pomeroy, Portland, Ore.	Cleveland, Ohio
1945	Jax Maids, New Orleans, La.	Cleveland, Ohio
1946	Jax Maids, New Orleans, La.	Cleveland, Ohio
1947	Jax Maids, New Orleans, La.	Cleveland, Ohio
1948	Arizona Ramblers, Phoenix, Ariz.	Portland, Ore.
1949	Arizona Ramblers, Phoenix, Ariz.	Portland, Ore.
1950	Orange Lionettes, Orange, Cal.	San Antonio, Tex.
1951	Orange Lionettes, Orange, Cal.	Detroit, Mich.
1952	Orange Lionettes, Orange, Cal.	Toronto, Canada
1953	Betsy Ross Rockets, Fresno, Cal.	Toronto, Canada
1954	Leach Motor Rockets, Fresno, Cal.	Orange, Cal.
1955	Orange Lionettes, Orange, Cal.	Portland, Ore.
1956	Orange Lionettes, Orange, Cal.	Clearwater, Fla.
1957	Hacienda Rockets, Fresno, Cal.	Bueno Park, Cal.
1958	Raybestos Brakettes, Stratford, Conn.	Stratford, Conn.
1959	Raybestos Brakettes, Stratford, Conn.	Stratford, Conn.
1960	Raybestos Brakettes, Stratford, Conn.	Stratford, Conn.
1961	Gold Sox, Whittier, Cal.	Portland, Ore.
1962	Orange Lionettes, Orange, Cal.	Stratford, Conn.
1963	Raybestos Brakettes, Stratford, Conn.	Stratford, Conn.
1964	Erv Lind Florists, Portland, Ore.	Orlando, Fla.
1965	Orange Lionettes, Orange, Cal.	Stratford, Conn.
1966	Raybestos Brakettes, Stratford, Conn.	Orlando, Fla.
1967	Raybestos Brakettes, Stratford, Conn.	Stratford, Conn.
1968	Raybestos Brakettes, Stratford, Conn.	Stratford, Conn.
1969	Orange Lionettes, Orange, Cal.	Tucson, Ariz.
1970	Orange Lionettes, Orange, Cal.	Stratford, Conn.
1971	Raybestos Brakettes, Stratford, Conn.	Orlando, Fla.
1972	Raybestos Brakettes, Stratford, Conn.	Tucson, Ariz.
1973	Raybestos Brakettes, Stratford, Conn.	Stratford, Conn.
1974	Raybestos Brakettes, Stratford, Conn.	Orlando, Fla.
1975	Raybestos Brakettes, Stratford, Conn.	Salt Lake City, Utah
1976	Raybestos Brakettes, Stratford, Conn.	Stratford, Conn.
1977	Raybestos Brakettes, Stratford, Conn.	Hayward, Cal.
1978	Raybestos Brakettes, Stratford, Conn.	Allentown, Pa.

The 1978 Raybestos Brakettes fast pitch softball team continued the Stratford, Connecticut team's winning tradition by posting their eighth consecutive national championship.

Women's Major Fast Pitch National Tournament Records

Batting, Individual

Highest Average: .632 by Diane Kalliam (Santa Clara, Cal.) in 1975

Most Hits: 14 by Pat Guenzler (St. Louis, Mo.) in 1975

Most Home Runs: 4 by Robbie Mulkey (Portland, Ore.) in 1949

Most Triples: 3 by four players; Irene Huber (Fresno, Cal.) in 1949, Lu Flanagan (Seattle, Ore.) in 1971, Lana Svec (Ashland, Ohio) in 1977, and Marilyn Rau (Sun City, Ariz.) in 1978

Most Doubles: 5 by two players; Joan Joyce (Stratford, Conn.) in 1968, and Barbara Reinalda (Stratford) in 1976

Most RBI's: 10 by Kay Rich (Fresno, Cal.) in 1955

Most Runs Scored: 9 by Irene Shea (Stratford) in 1975

Batting, Team

Most Hits: 69 by Stratford in 1974

Most Home Runs: 4 by Portland in 1949

Most Triples: 7 by two teams; Phoenix, Ariz. in 1955, and Ashland, Ohio in 1977

Most Doubles: 12 by Stratford in 1968

Most RBI's: 30 by Fresno in 1955

Pitching, Individual

Most Innings Pitched: 70 by Joan Joyce (Stratford) in 1974

Most Strikeouts: 134 by Joan Joyce (Stratford) in 1973

Most Strikeouts (Game): 20 by Bertha Tickey (Orange, Cal.) in 1953 (7 innings); 40 by Joan Joyce (Stratford) in 1961 (18 innings)

Most No-Hit Games: 3 by Louise Mazzucca (Portland, Ore.) in 1960

Most Perfect Games: 3 by Bertha Tickey (Orange-Stratford) in 1950, 54, 68

Most National Tournament Wins: 69 by Bertha Tickey (Stratford) in 19 national tournaments

Most Consecutive Strikeouts: 11 by Bertha Tickey (Stratford) in 1968

Team Championships

Most Consecutive National Championships: 8 by Stratford

Most National Championships, Total: 15 by Stratford

National Women's Major Slow Pitch Championship

Year	Champions	Tournament Location
1961	Dairy Cottage, Covington, Ky.	Cincinnati, Ohio
1962	Dana Gardens, Cincinnati, Ohio	Cincinnati, Ohio
1963	Dana Gardens, Cincinnati, Ohio	Cincinnati, Ohio
1964	Dana Gardens, Cincinnati, Ohio	Omaha, Neb.
1965	Art's Aces, Omaha, Neb.	Omaha, Neb.
1966	Dana Gardens, Cincinnati, Ohio	Burlington, N.C.
1967	Ridge Maintenance, Cleveland, Ohio	Sheboygan, Wis.
1968	Escue Pontiac, Cincinnati, Ohio	Cincinnati, Ohio

Year			
1969	Converse Dots, Hialeah, Fla.		Chattanooga, Tenn.
1970	Rutenschroer Floral, Cincinnati, Ohio		Parma, Ohio
1971	Gators, Ft. Lauderdale, Fla.		Satellite Beach, Fla.
1972	Riverside Ford, Cincinnati, Ohio		York, Pa.
1973	Sweeney Chevrolet, Cincinnati, Ohio		Chattanooga, Tenn.
1974	Marks Bros., N. Miami Dots, Miami, Fla.		Elk Grove, Cal.
1975	Marks Bros., N. Miami Dots, Miami, Fla.		Jacksonville, Fla.
1976	Sorrento's Pizza, Cincinnati, Ohio		Chattanooga, Tenn.
1977	Fox Valley Lassies, St. Charles, Ill.		Graham, N.C.
1978	Bob Hoffman's Dots, Miami, Fla.		Jacksonville, Fla.

Women's World Championship

Year	Champions	Tournament Location
1965	Australia	Melbourne, Australia
1970	Japan	Osaka, Japan
1974	U.S.	Stratford, Conn.
1978	U.S.	Japan

Women's World Championship Records

Most Runs: 13 by Elliott (U.S.) in 1974

Most Hits: 17 by Naruse (Japan) in 1974

Most RBI's: 11 by three players; Naruse (Japan), Usui (Japan), and Elliott (U.S.), all in 1974

Highest Batting Average: .515 by Naruse (Japan)

Most Wins, Pitching: 6 by two players; Wooley (Australia) in 1965, and Welborn (U.S.) in 1970

Most Innings Pitched: 50 by Welborn (U.S.) in 1970

Most Strikeouts: 76 by Joyce (U.S.) in 1974

Most Perfect Games: 2 by Joyce (U.S.) in 1974

Squash

Although racquets with a soft ball was evolved *c.*1850 at Harrow School, England, there was no recognized champion of any country until John A. Miskey of Philadelphia won the American Amateur Singles Championship in 1906.

Most Women's Titles

The greatest number of wins in the Women's Squash Rackets Championship is 16 by Heather Pamela McKay (*née* Blundell) (born Australia, July 31, 1941) between 1961 and 1976.

Shortest Championship Match

Sue Cogswell beat Teresa Lawes in only 16 minutes in a British Women's title match at Dallington, England, on December 12, 1977.

Heather McKay won 16 world championships in the years 1961–76.

Surfing

The traditional Polynesian sport of surfing in a canoe (*ehorooe*) was first recorded by Captain James Cook (1728–79) on his first voyage to Tahiti in December, 1771. Surfing on a board (*Amo Amo iluna ka lau oka nalu*) was first described ("most perilous and extraordinary . . . altogether astonishing and scarcely to be credited") by Lt. (later Capt.) James King in March, 1779, at Kealakekua Bay, Hawaii Island.

The sport was revived at Waikiki by 1900. Hollow boards were introduced in 1929, and the light plastic foam type in 1956.

World Championship

World Championships were inaugurated in 1964 in Sydney, Australia. The only surfer to win two titles has been Joyce Hoffman of the U.S., in 1965 and 1966.

Swimming

Swimming in schools in Japan was ordered by Imperial edict of Emperor Go-Yoozei as early as 1603, but competition was known from 36 B.C. Sea water bathing was fashionable at Scarborough, North Yorkshire, England, as early as 1660. Competitive swimming originated in London c.1837, at which time there were five or more pools in the city.

The first recorded women's world swimming record was set by Martha Gerstung of Germany in 100 meter freestyle competition in 1908. Women's swimming and diving were first included in the Olympic Games in 1912, when Fanny Durack of Australia took the gold medal in the 100 meter freestyle event with a time of 1 minute 22.2 seconds. World championship competition was instituted in 1973, and has been held twice since then.

Most World Records

The greatest number of world records held by any swimmer is 42 by Ragnhild Hveger of Denmark (born December 10, 1920), set between 1936 and 1942. The nearest male record-holder is Arne Borg of Sweden, who set 32 new world marks, from 1921–29.

Most Olympic Medals

The record number of Olympic gold medals won by a woman is 4, a feat which has been equalled by three women, as follows:

Patricia McCormick (*née* Keller), U.S., born May 12, 1930. Won High Diving in 1952 and 1956 along with Springboard Diving in the same years. She holds the record for individual gold medals.

Patricia McCormick has won two Olympic medals in each of the competitive diving events, springboard diving and high diving.

Kornelia Ender won four gold medals at the 1976 Olympics, setting Olympic records in each event and world records in three.

Dawn Fraser (later Mrs. Gary Ware), Australia, born September 4, 1937. Won 100 meter freestyle in three successive Olympics (1956–60–64) and 4 × 100 meter freestyle relay in 1956. She is the only swimmer to win the same event on three successive occasions.

Kornelia Ender, East Germany, born October 25, 1958. Won 100 meter and 200 meter freestyle, 100 meter butterfly and 4 × 100 meter medley relay, all at the 1976 Games.

The most total medals won by a woman is 8, accomplished by each of the following three women:

Dawn Fraser (see above), who in addition to her 4 golds won 4 silvers, in the 400 meter freestyle in 1956, 4 × 100 freestyle relay in 1960–64, and 4 × 100 medley relay in 1960.

Shirley Babashoff, U.S., born January 3, 1957. Won 2 golds in the 4 × 100 meter freestyle relay, 1972–76, along with 6 silvers, in the 100 meter freestyle in 1972, 200 meter freestyle in 1972–76, 400 meter and 800 meter freestyle in 1976, and 400 meter medley relay in 1976.

Kornelia Ender (see above), who, in addition to her 4 golds, won 4 silvers, in the 200 meter individual medley in 1972, 400 meter medley relay in 1972, and the 400 meter freestyle relay in 1972 and 1976.

Women's swimming was first included on the Olympic schedule in 1912, when Fanny Durack won the gold medal.

OLYMPIC GOLD MEDALISTS

100 Meter Freestyle

1912 Fanny Durack, Australasia	1952 Katalin Szoke, Hungary
1920 Ethelda M. Bleibtrey, U.S.	1956 Dawn Fraser, Australia
1924 Ethel Lackie, U.S.	1960 Dawn Fraser, Australia
1928 Albina Osipowich, U.S.	1964 Dawn Fraser, Australia
1932 Helene Madison, U.S.	1968 Jan M. Henne, U.S.
1936 Hendrika W. Mastenbroek, Neth.	1972 Sandra Neilson, U.S.
1948 Greta M. Andersen, Denmark	1976 Kornelia Ender, E. Germany

Olympic Record: 55.65 seconds by Kornelia Ender, 1976.

200 Meter Freestyle

1968 Debbie Meyer, U.S.	1976 Kornelia Ender, E. Germany
1972 Shane E. Gould, Australia	

Olympic Record: 1 minute 59.26 seconds by Kornelia Ender, 1976.

400 Meter Freestyle

1924	Martha Norelius, U.S.	1960	S. Christine von Saltza, U.S.
1928	Martha Norelius, U.S.		
1932	Helene Madison, U.S.	1964	Virginia Duenkel, U.S.
1936	Hendrika W. Mastenbroek, Neth.	1968	Debbie Meyer, U.S.
		1972	Shane E. Gould, Australia
1948	Ann E. Curtis, U.S.	1976	Petra Thuemer, E. Germany
1952	Valeria Gyenge, Hungary		
1956	Lorraine J. Crapp, Australia		

Olympic Record: 4 minutes 9.89 seconds by Petra Thuemer, 1976.

800 Meter Freestyle

1968	Debbie Meyer, U.S.	1976	Petra Thuemer, E. Germany
1972	Keena Rothhammer, U.S.		

Olympic Record: 8 minutes 37.14 seconds by Petra Thuemer, 1976.

100 Meter Backstroke

1924	Sybil Bauer, U.S.	1956	Judith B. Grinham, G.B.
1928	Marie J. Braun, Netherlands	1960	Lynn E. Burke, U.S.
		1964	Cathy Ferguson, U.S.
1932	Eleanor Holm, U.S.	1968	Kaye Hall, U.S.
1936	Dina W. J. Senff, Netherlands	1972	Melissa Belote, U.S.
		1976	Ulrike Richter, E. Germany
1948	Karen M. Harup, Denmark		
1952	Joan C. Harrison, South Africa		

Olympic Record: 1 minute 1.83 seconds by Ulrike Richter, 1976.

Shane Gould entered six events in the 1972 Olympics and won medals in five of them.

200 Meter Backstroke

1968 Lillian D. Watson, U.S.   1976 Ulrike Richter,
1972 Melissa Belote, U.S.   E. Germany

Olympic Record: 2 minutes 13.43 seconds by Ulrike Richter, 1976.

100 Meter Breaststroke

1968 Djurdjica Bjedov,   1976 Hannelore Anke,
       Yugoslavia   E. Germany
1972 Catherine Carr, U.S.

Olympic Record: 1 minute 10.86 seconds set by Anke in preliminary heat, 1976.

200 Meter Breaststroke

1924 Lucy Morton, G.B.   1964 Galina Prozumenshchi-
1928 Hilde Scrader, Germany   kova, U.S.S.R.
1932 Claire Dennis, Australia   1968 Sharon Wichman, U.S.
1936 Hideko Machata, Japan   1972 Beverly J. Whitfield,
1948 Petronella van Vliet, Neth.   Australia
1952 Eva Szekely, Hungary   1976 Marina Koshevaia,
1956 Ursula Happe, Germany   U.S.S.R.
1960 Anita Lonsbrough, G.B.

Olympic Record: 2 minutes 33.35 seconds by Marina Koshevaia, 1976.

Sharon Wichman overtaking defending Olympic medalist Galina Prozumenshchikova in the 1968 200 meter breaststroke event.

The 200 meter butterfly was a new event in the 1968 Games at Mexico City, where Aagje Kok won the gold medal.

100 Meter Butterfly

1956 Shelley Mann, U.S.
1960 Carolyn J. Schuler, U.S.
1964 Sharon Stouder, U.S.
1968 Lynette McClements,
    Australia

1972 Mayumi Aoki, Japan
1976 Kornelia Ender,
    E. Germany

Olympic Record: 1 minute 0.13 seconds by Kornelia Ender, 1976.

200 Meter Butterfly

1968 Aagje Kok, Netherlands
1972 Karen Moe, U.S.

1976 Andrea Pollack,
    E. Germany

Olympic Record: 2 minutes 11.41 seconds by Andrea Pollack, 1976.

400 Meter Individual Medley

1964 Donna De Varona, U.S.
1968 Claudia A. Kolb, U.S.
1972 Gail Neall, Australia

1976 Ulrike Tauber,
    E. Germany

Olympic Record: 4 minutes 42.77 seconds by Ulrike Tauber, 1976.

4 x 100 Meter Freestyle Relay

1912	Great Britain	1952	Hungary
1920	U.S.	1956	Australia
1924	U.S.	1960	U.S.
1928	U.S.	1964	U.S.
1932	U.S.	1968	U.S.
1936	Netherlands	1972	U.S.
1948	U.S.	1976	U.S.

Olympic Record: 3 minutes 44.82 seconds by U.S. team (Kim Peyton, Wendy Boglioli, Jill Sterkel, Shirley Babashoff), 1976.

4 x 100 Meter Medley Relay

1960	U.S.	1972	U.S.
1964	U.S.	1976	E. Germany
1968	U.S.		

Olympic Record: 4 minutes 7.95 seconds by East German team (Ulrike Richter, Hannelore Anke, Andrea Pollack, Kornelia Ender), 1976.

Shirley Babashoff holds a total of 8 Olympic medals, including 2 golds in the 4 × 100 meter freestyle relay (1972 and 1976).

Springboard Diving

1920	Aileen M. Riggin, U.S.	1936	Marjorie Gestring, U.S.
1924	Elizabeth Becker, U.S.	1948	Victoria Draves, U.S.
1928	Helen Meany, U.S.	1952	Patricia McCormick, U.S.
1932	Georgia Coleman, U.S.	1956	Patricia McCormick, U.S.

Jennifer Chandler's 1976 gold medal gave the U.S. the Springboard Diving title for the eleventh time.

1960	Ingrid Krämer, W. Germany	1968	Sue Gossick, U.S.
1964	Ingrid Engel, W. Germany	1972	Micki J. King, U.S.
		1976	Jennifer Chandler, U.S.

Platform Diving

1912	Greta Johansson, Sweden	1956	Patricia McCormick, U.S.
1920	Stefani Fryland-Clausen, Denmark	1960	Ingrid Krämer, W. Germany
1924	Caroline Smith, U.S.	1964	Lesley Bush, U.S.
1928	Elizabeth Pinkston, U.S.	1968	Milena Duchkova, Czech.
1932	Dorothy Poynton, U.S.	1972	Ulrika Knape, Sweden
1936	Dorothy Hill, U.S.	1976	Elena Vaytsekhovskaya, U.S.S.R.
1948	Victoria Draves, U.S.		
1952	Patricia McCormick, U.S.		

Women's World Swimming Records

The following are the official world records as recognized by the Federation Internationale de Natation as of August 24, 1978. Only performances set up in 50 meter pools are recognized as world records.

Freestyle

Event	min:sec	
100 meters	55.41	Barbara Krause (E. Germany), East Berlin, E. Germany, July 5, 1978
200 meters	1:58.53	Cynthia Woodhead (U.S.), West Berlin, W. Germany, August 22, 1978
400 meters	4:06.28	Tracey Wickham (Australia), West Berlin, W. Germany, August 24, 1978
800 meters	8:24.62	Tracey Wickham (Australia), Edmonton, Canada, August 5, 1978
1,500 meters	16:06.63	Tracey Wickham (Australia), Perth, W. Australia, February 24, 1979
4 × 100 m relay	3:43.43	U.S. National Team (Tracy Caulkins, Stephanie Elkins, Jill Sterkel, Cynthia Woodhead), West Berlin, W. Germany, August 27, 1978

Backstroke

Event	min:sec	
100 meters	1:01.51	Ulrike Richter (E. Germany), East Berlin, E. Germany, June 5, 1976
200 meters	2:11.93	Linda Jezek (U.S.), West Berlin, W. Germany, August 24, 1978

Breaststroke

Event	min:sec	
100 meters	1:10.31	Julia Bogdanova (U.S.S.R.), West Berlin, W. Germany, August 22, 1978
200 meters	2:31.42	Lina Kachushite (U.S.S.R.), West Berlin, W. Germany, August 24, 1978

Butterfly Stroke

Event	min:sec	
100 meters	59.46	Andrea Pollack (E. Germany), East Berlin, E. Germany, July 3, 1978

The 100 meter backstroke record set by Ulrike Richter in June, 1976, still stands, despite repeated challenges.

| 200 meters | 2:09.87 | Andrea Pollack (E. Germany), East Berlin, E. Germany, July 4, 1978 |
| | 2:09.87 | Tracy Caulkins (U.S.), West Berlin, W. Germany, August 26, 1978 |

Individual Medley

Event	min:sec	
200 meters	2:14.07	Tracy Caulkins (U.S.), West Berlin, W. Germany, August 20, 1978
400 meters	4:40.83	Tracy Caulkins (U.S.), West Berlin, W. Germany, August 23, 1978

Medley Relay

(Backstroke, Breaststroke, Butterfly Stroke, Freestyle)

| 4 × 100 meters | 4:07.95 | East German National Team (Ulrike Richter, Hannelore Anke, Andrea Pollack, Kornelia Ender), Montreal, Canada, July 18, 1976 |

U.S. Women's Swimming Records

The following are the American women's swimming records at metric distances accepted by the Amateur Athletic Union as of August 1, 1978. A.A.U. competition is held in two different categories related to pool size; the short course events take place in pools at least 25 yards but no more than 50 yards long, the long course in pools at least 50 yards long. The A.A.U. continues to keep records for non-metric distances in short course events only.

Freestyle

Event	min:sec	
100 meters		
Short Course	55.00	Stephanie Elkins (U.S.), Austin, Texas, April 16, 1978
Long Course	56.26	Wendy Boglioli (U.S.), East Berlin, E. Germany, August 27, 1977
200 meters		
Short Course	1:56.87	Cynthia Woodhead (U.S.), Austin, Texas, April 15, 1978
Long Course	1:58.53	Cynthia Woodhead (U.S.), West Berlin, W. Germany, August 22, 1978 (World Record)
400 meters		
Short Course	4:02.59	Cynthia Woodhead (U.S.), Austin, Texas, April 16, 1978
Long Course	4:07.15	Cynthia Woodhead (Riverside A.A.), West Berlin, W. Germany, August 24, 1978
800 meters		
Short Course	8:24.65	Cynthia Woodhead (U.S.), Austin, Texas, April 15, 1978
Long Course	8:29.35	Cynthia Woodhead (U.S.), West Berlin, W. Germany, August 28, 1978
1,500 meters		
Short Course	16:54.60	Deborah Meyer (Arden Hills Swim Club), Cincinnati, Ohio, April 12, 1970
Long Course	16:15.66	Kimberly A. Linehan (Sarasota "Y" S.), Mission Viejo, California, June 25, 1978
4 × 50 m Freestyle Relay		
Short Course	1:53.45	St. Petersburg Recreation Dept. (Dea Mignon Loy, Kimberly Jacobs, Jacqueline Bajus, Judith Ann Merrill), Sarasota, Florida, July 7, 1974

Long Course	1:49.06	U.S. National Team (Kathy Heddy, Kelly Rowell, Karen Reeser, Shirley Babashoff), Mission Viejo, California, July 12, 1975
4 × 100 m Freestyle Relay		
Short Course	3:43.88	U.S. National Team (Stephanie Elkins, Kelly Asplund, Jill Sterkel, Tracy Caulkins), Austin, Texas, April 15, 1978
Long Course	3:43.43	U.S. National Team (Tracy Caulkins, Stephanie Elkins, Jill Sterkel, Cynthia Woodhead), West Berlin, W. Germany, August 26, 1978 (World Record)

Backstroke

Event	min:sec	
100 meters		
Short Course	1:01.94	Linda Jezek (U.S.), Austin, Texas, April 16, 1978
Long Course	1:02.55	Linda Jezek (U.S.), West Berlin, W. Germany, August 22, 1978
200 meters		
Short Course	2:11.02	Linda Jezek (U.S.), Austin, Texas, April 15, 1978
Long Course	2:11.93	Linda Jezek (U.S.), West Berlin, W. Germany, August 24, 1978 (World Record)

Breaststroke

Event	min:sec	
100 meters		
Short Course	1:09.16	Tracy Caulkins (U.S.), Austin, Texas, April 16, 1978
Long Course	1:10.77	Tracy Caulkins (U.S.), West Berlin, W. Germany, August 22, 1978
200 meters		
Short Course	2:29.62	Tracy Caulkins (U.S.), Austin, Texas, April 15, 1978
Long Course	2:35.23	Tracy Caulkins (Nashville A.C.), Mission Viejo, California, June 25, 1978

Butterfly

Event	min:sec	
100 meters		
Short Course	1:00.73	Diane Johannigman (U.S.), Austin, Texas, April 16, 1978

| Long Course | 1:00.20 | Joan Pennington (U.S.), West Berlin, W. Germany, August 23, 1978 |

200 meters

| Short Course | 2:09.10 | Nancy Hogshead (U.S.), Austin, Texas, April 15, 1978 |
| Long Course | 2:09.87 | Tracy Caulkins (U.S.), West Berlin, W. Germany, August 26, 1978 (World Record) |

Individual Medley

| *Event* | *min:sec* | |

200 meters

| Short Course | 2:13.37 | Tracy Caulkins (U.S.), Austin, Texas, April 16, 1978 |
| Long Course | 2:14.07 | Tracy Caulkins (U.S.), West Berlin, W. Germany, August 20, 1978 (World Record) |

400 meters

| Short Course | 4:43.47 | Tracy Caulkins (U.S.), Austin, Texas, April 15, 1978 |
| Long Course | 4:40.83 | Tracy Caulkins (U.S.), West Berlin, W. Germany, August 23, 1978 (World Record) |

Medley Relay

| *Event* | *min:sec* | |

200 meters

| Short Course | 2:03.00 | U.S. National Team (Sara James, Allison Grant, Camille Wright, Diane Gentes), Port of Spain, Trinidad, September 1, 1973 |
| Long Course | 2:01.86 | U.S. National Team (Linda Jezek, Marcia Morey, Camille Wright, Bonny Brown), Mission Viejo, California, July 12, 1975 |

400 meters

| Short Course | 4:10.66 | U.S. National Team (Linda Jezek, Tracy Caulkins, Diane Johannigman, Stephanie Elkins), Austin, Texas, April 16, 1978 |
| Long Course | 4:08.21 | U.S. National Team (Linda Jezek, Tracy Caulkins, Joan Pennington, Cynthia Woodhead), West Berlin, W. Germany, August 20, 1978 |

Women's World Championship

FREESTYLE

100 Meters

1973 Kornelia Ender,
E. Germany
1975 Kornelia Ender,
E. Germany
1978 Barbara Krause,
E. Germany

200 Meters

1973 Keena Rothhammer, U.S.
1975 Shirley Babashoff, U.S.
1978 Cynthia Woodhead, U.S.

400 Meters

1973 Heather Greenwood, U.S.
1975 Shirley Babashoff, U.S.
1978 Tracey Wickham, Australia

800 Meters

1973 Novella Calligaris, Italy
1975 Jenny Turrall, Australia
1978 Tracey Wickham, Australia

BACKSTROKE

100 Meters

1973 Ulrike Richter,
E. Germany
1975 Ulrike Richter,
E. Germany
1978 Linda Jezek, U.S.

200 Meters

1973 Melissa Belote, U.S.
1975 Birgit Treiber, E. Germany
1978 Linda Jezek, U.S.

BREASTSTROKE

100 Meters

1973 Renate Vogel, E. Germany
1975 Hannelore Anke,
E. Germany
1978 Linda Kachushite,
U.S.S.R.

200 Meters

1973 Renate Vogel, E. Germany
1975 Hannelore Anke,
E. Germany
1978 Julia Bogdanova,
U.S.S.R.

BUTTERFLY

100 Meters

1973 Kornelia Ender,
E. Germany
1975 Kornelia Ender,
E. Germany
1978 Mary-Joan Pennington,
U.S.

200 Meters

1973 Rosemarie Kother.
E. Germany
1975 Rosemarie Kother,
E. Germany
1978 Tracy Caulkins, U.S.

INDIVIDUAL MEDLEY

200 Meters

1973 Angela Hubner,
     E. Germany
1975 Kathy Heddy, U.S.
1978 Tracy Caulkins, U.S.

400 Meters

1973 Gudrun Wegner,
     E. Germany
1975 Ulrike Tauber,
     E. Germany
1978 Tracy Caulkins, U.S.

RELAYS

4 x 100 Meters Freestyle

1973 E. Germany
1975 E. Germany
1978 U.S.

4 x 100 Meters Medley

1973 E. Germany
1975 E. Germany
1978 U.S.

DIVING

Springboard

1973 Christine Kohler,
     E. Germany
1975 Irina Kalinina, U.S.S.R.
1978 Irina Kalinina, U.S.S.R.

Platform (High board)

1973 Ulrike Knape, Sweden
1975 Janet Ely, U.S.
1978 Irina Kalinina, U.S.S.R.

SYNCHRONIZED SWIMMING

Solo

1973 Teresa Andersen, U.S.
1975 Gail Buzonas, U.S.
1978 Helen Vanderburg,
     Canada

Duet

1973 U.S.
1975 U.S.
1978 Canada

Team

1973 U.S.
1975 U.S.
1978 U.S.

English Channel

The first man to swim across the English Channel (without a life-jacket) was the merchant navy captain Matthew Webb, who swam breaststroke from Dover, England, to Cap Gris-Nez, France, in 21 hours 45 minutes on August 24–25, 1875. Webb swam an estimated 38 miles to make the 21-mile crossing. The

Two of the most successful challengers of the English Channel have been Cindy Nicholas (above), who completed a double crossing in less than 20 hours in 1977, and Gertrude Ederle (right), the first woman Channel swimmer, who made the trip in August 1926.

first crossing from France to England was made by Enrique Tiraboschi, a wealthy Italian living in Argentina, who crossed in 16 hours 33 minutes on August 11, 1923, to win a $5,000 prize.

The first woman to succeed was Gertrude Ederle (U.S.) who swam from Cap Gris-Nez, France, to Dover, England, on August 6, 1926, in the then record time of 14 hours 39 minutes. The first woman to swim from England to France was Florence Chadwick of California, in 16 hours 19 minutes on September 11, 1951. She repeated this on September 4, 1953, and October 12, 1955.

Youngest and Oldest

The youngest woman to conquer the channel was Abla Adel Khairi (born in Egypt, September 26, 1960), aged 13 years 10 months when she swam from England to France in 12 hours 30 minutes on August 17, 1974. The oldest was Stella Taylor (born in U.S., December 20, 1929), aged 45 years 8 months when she swam it in 18 hours 15 minutes on August 26, 1975.

Fastest

The fastest crossing of the English Channel by either sex was made by an American woman, Penny Dean (born March 21, 1955), who swam from Shakespeare Beach, Dover to Cap Gris-Nez, France in 7 hours 40 minutes on July 29, 1978.

Fastest Double Crossing

Cynthia Nicholas, a 19-year-old from Canada, became the first woman to complete a double crossing of the English Channel, September 7–8, 1977. Her astonishing time of 19 hours 55 minutes set a new all-time mark, more than 10 hours faster than the previous male record holder.

Table Tennis

The earliest evidence relating to a game resembling table tennis has been found in the catalogues of London sporting goods manufacturers in the 1880's. The old Ping-Pong Association was formed there in 1902, but the game proved only a temporary craze until resuscitated in 1921.

Youngest International

The youngest ever international was Joy Foster, aged 8, the 1958 Jamaican singles and mixed doubles champion. This is probably the record for either sex in any sport.

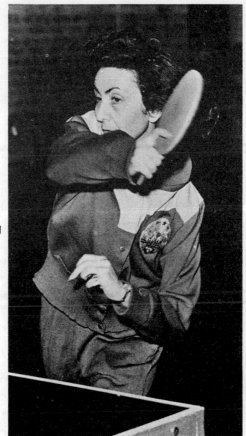

Angelica Rozeanu won the women's singles championship for six consecutive years beginning in 1950.

Most World Championship Wins

The greatest number of wins in the women's singles competition, held since 1927 for the G. Geist Prize, is six by Angelica Rozeanu of Rumania, who won consecutive titles, 1950–55.

Competition for the women's doubles title, the W. J. Pope Trophy, has been held since 1928, with the most successful player being Maria Mednyanszky of Hungary, who won seven times with two different partners; Erika Flamm in 1928, Anna Sipos in 1930–35. Mednyanszky also holds the record for most wins in mixed doubles, with 6 wins with three different partners (1927, 28, 30, 31, 33, 34), and a record total of 18 personal titles.

Tennis

The modern game of lawn tennis is generally agreed to have evolved as an outdoor form of Royal Tennis. "Field Tennis" was mentioned in an English magazine on September 29, 1793. The earliest club for such a game, variously called Pelota or Lawn Rackets, was the Leamington Club, founded in 1872 in England. In February, 1874, Major Walter Clopton Wingfield patented a form called "sphairistike," but the game soon became known as lawn tennis.

Competition for the British Championship began at Wimbledon, England, in 1877, with men's singles only. Women's singles were added in 1884, and women's doubles and mixed doubles in 1913. The first non-British winner at Wimbledon was an American woman, May Sutton, who won the 1905 singles title.

Tennis was first brought to the U.S. by a woman, Mary Ewing Outerbridge of Staten Island, New York, who played the game in Bermuda in 1874, and was so taken with it that she brought rackets, nets and balls back to her home and introduced the game to her friends. The first court on American soil was set up in the spring of 1874 on the grounds of the Staten Island Cricket and Baseball Club. One of the directors of the club was Miss Outerbridge's brother.

The United States National Lawn Tennis Association, later called the U.S. Lawn Tennis Association and, since 1975, the U.S. Tennis Association, was founded in 1881. They organized the first national championships in that year, with competition in men's singles and doubles at Newport, Rhode Island. Women's singles was added in 1887, and doubles in 1890. The tournament was moved to Forest Hills, New York, in 1915, where it remained until 1978, when the national championships were played at the U.S.T.A. National Tennis Center at Flushing Meadows, Queens, New York, for the first time.

Amateurs were permitted to play with and against professionals in Open tournaments starting in 1968.

Early women's tennis outfits were extremely restricting, as illustrated by these examples from the 1880's.

Greatest Crowd

The greatest crowd at a tennis match was the 30,472 who came to the Houston Astrodome in Houston, Texas, on September 20, 1973, to watch Billie Jean King beat a man over 25 years her senior, Bobby Riggs, in straight sets in the so-called "Tennis Match of the Century." This does not begin to include the enormous international television audience for the highly publicized stunt.

Born Billie Jean Moffitt on November 22, 1943, Ms King has been the foremost driving force behind the movement towards

Billie Jean King was the first woman athlete to earn more than $100,000 in a single season ($117,400 in 1971), and the second (after Chris Evert) to earn $1,000,000 total.

parity with male athletes in professional sports. Along with her personal record-setting triumphs have been her organizational successes in founding and developing World Team Tennis and publishing *womenSports* magazine. More recently she has been involved in the establishment of a professional softball league for women. In 1978, she founded the Women's Sports Foundation, a non-profit organization to encourage and support women's participation in sports through education and provision of training and facilities for sportswomen. The foundation also publishes *Women's Sports* magazine, the successor to the earlier publication which folded in mid-1978.

Through her powerful media presence and outstanding professional accomplishments, Billie Jean King continues to serve as a catalyst for rapid positive change throughout the field of women's sports.

"Grand Slam"

The grand slam in tennis is to hold at the same time all four of the world's major championship singles titles: Wimbledon, the U.S. Open, the Australian Open and the French Open.

Two women have achieved this feat, Maureen Catherine Connolly (U.S.,1934–69) in 1953, and Margaret Court (*née* Smith) (Australia, born July 16, 1942) in 1970.

Olympic Medals

Lawn tennis for women was part of the Olympic program briefly at the turn of the century. The most medals won by a woman is five by Kitty McKane (later Mrs. L. A. Godfree) of Great Britain, with one gold, two silver and two bronze in 1920 and 1924. Five different women won a record two gold medals.

Wimbledon Records

Most Wins

Elizabeth (Bunny) Ryan (U.S., 1894–1979) won her first title in 1914 and her nineteenth in 1934. This total includes 12 women's doubles with 5 different partners and 7 mixed doubles with 5 different partners. Her total of 19 championships was exceeded by Billie Jean King with 6 singles, 10 women's doubles and 4 mixed doubles between 1961 and 1979.

Youngest Champion

The youngest champion ever at Wimbledon was Charlotte Dod (1871–1960), who was 15 years 9 months old when she won in 1887.

Maureen Connolly (left) was the first of only two women to win the grand slam, with all four major singles titles, in 1953. Margaret Court equaled this feat in 1970.

Tracy Austin, the youngest modern player to compete at Wimbledon, continues to score impressive victories over older, more experienced adversaries.

The youngest player ever at Wimbledon was reputedly Miss M. Klima (Austria), who was 13 years old in the 1907 singles competition. The youngest in modern times is Tracy Austin (U.S., born December 12, 1962) who was only 14 years 7 months old in the 1977 tournament.

Longest Wimbledon Finals

The longest final match in the women's singles final lasted 2 hours 25 minutes, comprising 46 games between Margaret Smith Court and Billie Jean King in July, 1970. Court was victorious, with scores of 14-12 and 11-9.

The longest women's doubles finals have lasted 38 games, which took place on two occasions. In 1933, Simone Mathieu and Elizabeth Ryan beat Freda James and Adeline Maud Yorke of Great Britain by scores of 6-2, 9-11, 6-4. In 1963, it took 38 games for Rosemary Casals and Billie Jean King to clinch the title against Maria Bueno and Nancy Richey. Their scores were 9-11, 6-4, 6-2.

From 1971 the tie-break system was introduced, which effectually prevents sets proceeding beyond a 17th game. i.e. 9-8.

Women at Wimbledon

Singles

1884 Maud Watson, G.B.
1885 Maud Watson, G.B.
1886 Blanche Bingley, G.B.
1887 Lottie Dod, G.B.
1888 Lottie Dod, G.B.
1889 Blanche Bingley Hillyard,
      G.B.
1890 Helena Rice, G.B.
1891 Lottie Dod, G.B.
1892 Lottie Dod, G.B.
1893 Lottie Dod, G.B.
1894 Blanche Bingley Hillyard,
      G.B.
1895 Charlotte Cooper, G.B.
1896 Charlotte Cooper, G.B.
1897 Blanche Bingley Hillyard,
      G.B.
1898 Charlotte Cooper, G.B.
1899 Blanche Bingley Hillyard,
      G.B.
1900 Blanche Bingley Hillyard.
      G.B.
1901 Charlotte Cooper Sterry,
      G.B.
1902 Muriel Robb, G.B.
1903 Dorothea K. Douglass,
      G.B.
1904 Dorothea K. Douglass,
      G.B.
1905 May G. Sutton, U.S.
1906 Dorothea K. Douglass,
      G.B.
1907 May G. Sutton, U.S.
1908 Charlotte Cooper Sterry,
      G.B.
1909 Penelope Boothby, G.B.
1910 Dorothea Douglass
      Chambers, G.B.
1911 Dorothea Douglass
      Chambers, G.B.
1912 Ethel W. Larcombe, G.B.
1913 Dorothea Douglass
      Chambers, G.B.

Maria Bueno won approximately 585 tournaments in a career which might have been even more formidable had she not developed severe elbow problems.

1914 Dorothea Douglass
      Chambers, G.B.
1915–1918 No competition
1919 Suzanne Lenglen, France
1920 Suzanne Lenglen, France
1921 Suzanne Lenglen, France
1922 Suzanne Lenglen, France
1923 Suzanne Lenglen, France
1924 Kathleen McKane, G.B.
1925 Suzanne Lenglen, France
1926 Kathleen McKane
      Godfree, G.B.
1927 Helen Wills, U.S.
1928 Helen Wills, U.S.
1929 Helen Wills, U.S.
1930 Helen Wills Moody, U.S.
1931 Cilly Aussem, Germany
1932 Helen Wills Moody, U.S.
1933 Helen Wills Moody, U.S.

Evonne Goolagong won over 80 per cent of her matches in 1973–78.

1939	Alice Marble, U.S.
1940–45	No competition
1946	Pauline M. Betz, U.S.
1947	Margaret E. Osborne, U.S.
1948	A. Louise Brough, U.S.
1949	A. Louise Brough, U.S.
1950	A. Louise Brough, U.S.
1951	Doris Hart, U.S.
1952	Maureen Connolly, U.S.
1953	Maureen Connolly, U.S.
1954	Maureen Connolly, U.S.
1955	A. Louise Brough, U.S.
1956	Shirley J. Fry, U.S.
1957	Althea Gibson, U.S.
1958	Althea Gibson, U.S.
1959	Maria Bueno, Brazil
1960	Maria Bueno, Brazil
1961	Angela Mortimer, G.B.
1962	Karen Hantze Susman, U.S.
1963	Margaret Smith, Australia
1964	Maria Bueno, Brazil
1965	Margaret Smith, Australia
1966	Billie Jean King, U.S.
1967	Billie Jean King, U.S.
1968	Billie Jean King, U.S.
1969	Ann Haydon Jones, G.B.
1970	Margaret Smith Court, Australia
1971	Evonne Goolagong, Australia
1972	Billie Jean King, U.S.
1973	Billie Jean King, U.S.
1974	Chris Evert, U.S.
1975	Billie Jean King, U.S.
1976	Chris Evert, U.S.
1977	Virginia Wade, G.B.
1978	Martina Navratilova, Czech.

1934	Dorothy E. Round, G.B.
1935	Helen Wills Moody, U.S.
1936	Helen Hull Jacobs, U.S.
1937	Dorothy E. Round, G.B.
1938	Helen Wills Moody, U.S.

Doubles

1913	Winifred McNair—Penelope Boothby
1914	Elizabeth Ryan—Agnes Morton
1915–18	No competition
1919	Suzanne Lenglen—Elizabeth Ryan
1920	Suzanne Lenglen—Elizabeth Ryan
1921	Suzanne Lenglen—Elizabeth Ryan

1922	Suzanne Lenglen—Elizabeth Ryan
1923	Suzanne Lenglen—Elizabeth Ryan
1924	Hazel Hotchkiss Wightman—Helen Wills
1925	Suzanne Lenglen—Elizabeth Ryan
1926	Elizabeth Ryan—Mary K. Browne
1927	Elizabeth Ryan—Helen Wills
1928	Phoebe Watson—Peggy Saunders
1929	Phoebe Watson—Peggy Saunders Michell
1930	Elizabeth Ryan—Helen Wills Moody
1931	Dorothy Shepherd-Barron—Phyllis Mudford
1932	Doris Metaxa—Josane Sigart
1933	Elizabeth Ryan—Rene Mathieu
1934	Elizabeth Ryan—Rene Mathieu
1935	Katherine E. Stammers—Freda James
1936	Katherine E. Stammers—Freda James
1937	Rene Mathieu—Adeline Yorke
1938	Alice Marble—Sarah Palfrey Fabyan
1939	Alice Marble—Sarah Palfrey Fabyan
1940–45	No competition
1946	A. Louise Brough—Margaret Osborne du Pont
1947	Doris Hart—Patricia Canning Todd
1948	A. Louise Brough—Margaret Osborne du Pont
1949	A. Louise Brough—Margaret Osborne du Pont
1950	A. Louise Brough—Margaret Osborne du Pont
1951	Doris Hart—Shirley J. Fry
1952	Doris Hart—Shirley J. Fry
1953	Doris Hart—Shirley J. Fry

Elizabeth "Bunny" Ryan won a total of 19 Wimbledon championships in 20 years of competition.

1954	A. Louise Brough—Margaret Osborne du Pont
1955	Angela Mortimer—Jacqueline Anne Shilcock
1956	Angela Buxton—Althea Gibson
1957	Althea Gibson—Darlene Hard
1958	Althea Gibson—Maria Bueno
1959	Jeanne Arth—Darlene Hard
1960	Maria Bueno—Darlene Hard
1961	Karen Hantze—Billie Jean Moffitt
1962	Karen Susman—Billie Jean Moffitt
1963	Maria Bueno—Darlene Hard
1964	Margaret Smith—Lesley Turner
1965	Maria Bueno—Billie Jean Moffitt
1966	Maria Bueno—Nancy Richey
1967	Rosemary Casals—Billie Jean King
1968	Rosemary Casals—Billie Jean King
1969	Margaret Smith Court—Judy Tegart
1970	Billie Jean King—Rosemary Casals
1971	Billie Jean King—Rosemary Casals
1972	Billie Jean King—Betty Stove
1973	Billie Jean King—Rosemary Casals
1974	Peggy Michel—Evonne Goolagong
1975	Kazuko Sawamatsu—Ann Kiyomura
1976	Chris Evert—Martina Navratilova
1977	Helen Cawley—Joanne Russell
1978	Kerry Reid—Wendy Turnbull

Betty Stove is one of only four women currently playing to have won doubles titles at Wimbledon, the U.S. Open and the French Open, all in 1972.

Mixed Doubles

The greatest number of mixed doubles wins at Wimbledon was seven by Elizabeth (Bunny) Ryan of the U.S., with five different partners: Randolph Lycett (1919, 21, 23), Francis T. Hunter (1927), P. D. B. Spence (1928), John H. Crawford (1930) and Enrique Maier (1932).

U.S. Tennis Association Women's Championships

Singles

1887 Ellen F. Hansell
1888 Bertha L. Townsend
1889 Bertha L. Townsend
1890 Ellen C. Roosevelt
1891 Mabel E. Cahill
1892 Mabel E. Cahill
1893 Aline M. Terry
1894 Helen R. Helwig
1895 Juliette P. Atkinson
1896 Elisabeth H. Moore
1897 Juliette P. Atkinson
1898 Juliette P. Atkinson
1899 Marion Jones
1900 Myrtle McAteer
1901 Elisabeth H. Moore
1902 Marion Jones
1903 Elisabeth H. Moore
1904 May G. Sutton
1905 Elisabeth H. Moore
1906 Helen Homans
1907 Evelyn Sears
1908 Maud Bargar-Wallach
1909 Hazel Hotchkiss
1910 Hazel Hotchkiss
1911 Hazel Hotchkiss
1912 Mary K. Browne
1913 Mary K. Browne
1914 Mary K. Browne
1915 Molla Bjurstedt
1916 Molla Bjurstedt
1917 Molla Bjurstedt
1918 Molla Bjurstedt
1919 Hazel Hotchkiss Wightman
1920 Molla Bjurstedt Mallory
1921 Molla Bjurstedt Mallory
1922 Molla Bjurstedt Mallory
1923 Helen Wills
1924 Helen Wills
1925 Helen Wills
1926 Molla Bjurstedt Mallory
1927 Helen Wills

Althea Gibson became the first black winner at Forest Hills with her 1957 singles victory.

1928 Helen Wills
1929 Helen Wills
1930 Betty Nuthall (G.B.)
1931 Helen Wills Moody
1932 Helen Hull Jacobs
1933 Helen Hull Jacobs
1934 Helen Hull Jacobs
1935 Helen Hull Jacobs
1936 Alice Marble
1937 Anita Lizana (Chile)
1938 Alice Marble
1939 Alice Marble
1940 Alice Marble
1941 Sarah Palfrey Cooke
1942 Pauline M. Betz
1943 Pauline M. Betz
1944 Pauline M. Betz
1945 Sarah Palfrey Cooke
1946 Pauline M. Betz
1947 A. Louise Brough

1948	Margaret Osborne du Pont	1964	Maria Bueno
1949	Margaret Osborne du Pont	1965	Margaret Smith
1950	Margaret Osborne du Pont	1966	Maria Bueno
1951	Maureen Connolly	1967	Billie Jean King
1952	Maureen Connolly	1968	Virginia Wade
1953	Maureen Connolly	1969	Margaret Smith Court
1954	Doris Hart	1970	Margaret Smith Court
1955	Doris Hart	1971	Billie Jean King
1956	Shirley J. Fry	1972	Billie Jean King
1957	Althea Gibson	1973	Margaret Smith Court
1958	Althea Gibson	1974	Billie Jean King
1959	Maria Bueno	1975	Chris Evert
1960	Darlene Hard	1976	Chris Evert
1961	Darlene Hard	1977	Chris Evert
1962	Margaret Smith	1978	Chris Evert
1963	Maria Bueno		

Doubles

1890	Ellen Roosevelt—Grace Roosevelt
1891	Mabel Cahill—W. Fellowes Morgan
1892	Mabel Cahill—A. M. McKinley
1893	Aline M. Terry—Hattie Butler
1894	Helen Helwig—Juliette P. Atkinson
1895	Helen Helwig—Juliette P. Atkinson
1896	Elisabeth Moore—Juliette P. Atkinson
1897	Juliette P. Atkinson—Kathleen Atkinson
1898	Juliette P. Atkinson—Kathleen Atkinson
1899	Jane W. Craven—Myrtle McAteer
1900	Edith Parker—Hallie Champlin
1901	Juliette P. Atkinson—Myrtle McAteer
1902	Juliette P. Atkinson—Marion Jones
1903	Elisabeth Moore—Carrie Neely
1904	May Sutton—Miriam Hall
1905	Helen Homans—Carrie Neely
1906	L. S. Cole—D. S. Platt
1907	Marie Weimer—Carrie Neely
1908	Evelyn Sears—Margaret Curtis
1909	Hazel Hotchkiss—Edith Rotch
1910	Hazel Hotchkiss—Edith Rotch
1911	Hazel Hotchkiss—Eleonora Sears
1912	Dorothy Green—Mary K. Browne
1913	Mary K. Browne—R. H. Williams
1914	Mary K. Browne—R. H. Williams
1915	Hazel Hotchkiss Wightman—Eleonora Sears
1916	Molla Bjurstedt—Eleonora Sears

1917	Molla Bjurstedt—Eleonora Sears
1918	Marion Zinderstein—Eleonor Goss
1919	Marion Zinderstein—Eleonor Goss
1920	Marion Zinderstein—Eleonor Goss
1921	Mary K. Browne—R. H. Williams
1922	Marion Zinderstein Jessup—Helen Wills
1923	Kathleen McKane—B. C. Covell (G.B.)
1924	Hazel Hotchkiss Wightman—Helen Wills
1925	Mary K. Browne—Helen Wills
1926	Elizabeth Ryan—Eleanor Goss
1927	Kathleen McKane Godfree—Ermyntrude H. Harvey (G.B.)
1928	Hazel Hotchkiss Wightman—Helen Wills
1929	Phoebe Watson—Peggy Saunders Michell
1930	Betty Nuthall (G.B.)—Sarah Palfrey
1931	Betty Nuthall—Eileen Bennett Whittingstall (G.B.)
1932	Helen Hull Jacobs—Sarah Palfrey
1933	Betty Nuthall—Freda James (G.B.)
1934	Helen Hull Jacobs—Sarah Palfrey
1935	Helen Hull Jacobs—Sarah Palfrey Fabyan
1936	Marjorie Gladman Van Ryn—Carolin Babcock
1937	Sarah Palfrey Fabyan—Alice Marble
1938	Sarah Palfrey Fabyan—Alice Marble
1939	Sarah Palfrey Fabyan—Alice Marble
1940	Sarah Palfrey—Alice Marble
1941	Sarah Palfrey Cooke—Margaret E. Osborne
1942	A. Louise Brough—Margaret E. Osborne
1943	A. Louise Brough—Margaret E. Osborne
1944	A. Louise Brough—Margaret E. Osborne
1945	A. Louise Brough—Margaret E. Osborne
1946	A. Louise Brough—Margaret E. Osborne
1947	A. Louise Brough—Margaret E. Osborne
1948	A. Louise Brough—Margaret Osborne du Pont
1949	A. Louise Brough—Margaret Osborne du Pont
1950	A. Louise Brough—Margaret Osborne du Pont
1951	Doris Hart—Shirley Fry
1952	Doris Hart—Shirley Fry
1953	Doris Hart—Shirley Fry
1954	Doris Hart—Shirley Fry
1955	A. Louise Brough—Margaret Osborne du Pont
1956	A. Louise Brough—Margaret Osborne du Pont
1957	A. Louise Brough—Margaret Osborne du Pont
1958	Jeanne Arth—Darlene Hard
1959	Jeanne Arth—Darlene Hard
1960	Maria Bueno—Darlene Hard
1961	Darlene Hard—Lesley Turner
1962	Maria Bueno—Darlene Hard
1963	Robyn Ebbern—Margaret Smith
1964	Billie Jean Moffitt—Karen Susman

1965	Carole Graebner—Nancy Richey
1966	Maria Bueno—Nancy Richey
1967	Billie Jean King—Rosemary Casals
1968	Margaret Smith Court—Maria Bueno
1969	Francoise Durr—Darlene Hard
1970	Margaret Smith Court—Judy Tegart Dalton
1971	Rosemary Casals—Judy Tegart Dalton
1972	Francoise Durr—Betty Stove
1973	Margaret Smith Court—Virginia Wade
1974	Billie Jean King—Rosemary Casals
1975	Margaret Smith Court—Virginia Wade
1976	Ilina Kloss—Linsky Boshoff
1977	Betty Stove—Martina Navratilova
1978	Billie Jean King—Martina Navratilova

Mixed Doubles

The greatest number of wins in the mixed doubles competition has been nine by Margaret Osborne du Pont of the U.S., with four different partners: William F. Talbert (1943–46), Kenneth McGregor (1950), Kenneth Rosewall (1956) and Neale Fraser (1958–60).

The powerful doubles team of Casals and King won the U.S. Open title in 1974, having already taken the Wimbledon title five times.

Hazel Wightman presents the cup bearing her name to the winning U.S. team in 1949. Team members are (left to right) Doris Hart, Beverley Baker, Mrs. Richard Buck, Patricia Todd, Gertrude "Gussie" Moran, Shirley Fry and Louise Brough.

Wightman Cup

Since 1923, women's tennis teams from the U.S. and Great Britain have met each year to vie for the Wightman Cup, donated by Hazel Hotchkiss Wightman (U.S., 1887–1974), who herself won 48 U.S. tennis titles between 1909 and 1954, including the U.S. national singles title in 1909–11. The first competition took place on August 11 and 13, 1923, at the West Side Tennis Club, Forest Hills, New York.

1923   U.S. defeated G.B. 7–0 at Forest Hills
1924   G.B. defeated U.S. 6–1 at Wimbledon, England
1925   G.B. defeated U.S. 4–3 at Forest Hills
1926   U.S. defeated G.B. 4–3 at Wimbledon
1927   U.S. defeated G.B. 5–2 at Forest Hills
1928   G.B. defeated U.S. 4–3 at Wimbledon
1929   U.S. defeated G.B. 4–3 at Forest Hills

1930 G.B. defeated U.S. 4–3 at Wimbledon
1931 U.S. defeated G.B. 5–2 at Forest Hills
1932 U.S. defeated G.B. 4–3 at Wimbledon
1933 U.S. defeated G.B. 4–3 at Forest Hills
1934 U.S. defeated G.B. 5–2 at Wimbledon
1935 U.S. defeated G.B. 4–3 at Forest Hills
1936 U.S. defeated G.B. 4–3 at Wimbledon
1937 U.S. defeated G.B. 6–1 at Forest Hills
1938 U.S. defeated G.B. 5–2 at Wimbledon
1939 U.S. defeated G.B. 5–2 at Forest Hills
1940–45 No competition
1946 U.S. defeated G.B. 7–0 at Wimbledon
1947 U.S. defeated G.B. 7–0 at Forest Hills
1948 U.S. defeated G.B. 6–1 at Wimbledon
1949 U.S. defeated G.B. 7–0 at Merion Cricket Club, Haverford, Pa.
1950 U.S. defeated G.B. 7–0 at Wimbledon
1951 U.S. defeated G.B. 6–1 at Longwood Cricket Club, Chestnut Hill, Mass.
1952 U.S. defeated G.B. 7–0 at Wimbledon
1953 U.S. defeated G.B. 7–0 at Rye, N.Y.
1954 U.S. defeated G.B. 6–0 at Wimbledon (Note: One doubles match was cancelled because of rain)
1955 U.S. defeated G.B. 6–1 at Rye
1956 U.S. defeated G.B. 5–2 at Wimbledon
1957 U.S. defeated G.B. 6–1 at Sewickley, Pa.
1958 G.B. defeated U.S. 4–3 at Wimbledon
1959 U.S. defeated G.B. 4–3 at Sewickley
1960 G.B. defeated U.S. 4–3 at Wimbledon
1961 U.S. defeated G.B. 6–1 at Chicago
1962 U.S. defeated G.B. 4–3 at Wimbledon
1963 U.S. defeated G.B. 6–1 at Cleveland
1964 U.S. defeated G.B. 5–2 at Wimbledon
1965 U.S. defeated G.B. 5–2 at Cleveland
1966 U.S. defeated G.B. 4–3 at Wimbledon
1967 U.S. defeated G.B. 6–1 at Cleveland
1968 G.B. defeated U.S. 4–3 at Wimbledon
1969 U.S. defeated G.B. 5–2 at Cleveland
1970 U.S. defeated G.B. 4–3 at Wimbledon
1971 U.S. defeated G.B. 4–3 at Cleveland
1972 U.S. defeated G.B. 5–2 at Wimbledon
1973 U.S. defeated G.B. 5–2 at Longwood
1974 G.B. defeated U.S. 6–1 at Deeside, Wales
1975 G.B. defeated U.S. 5–2 at Cleveland
1976 U.S. defeated G.B. 5–2 at London
1977 U.S. defeated G.B. 7–0 at Oakland, Ca.
1978 G.B. defeated U.S. 4–3 at London

Series to date: U.S. has won 40 times, G.B. 10 times.

Federation Cup

Inaugurated in 1963 by the International Lawn Tennis Federation to celebrate the fiftieth anniversary of the organization's founding, the Federation Cup attracts women's teams from over 20 countries.

1963	U.S. defeated Australia 2–1 at London, England
1964	Australia defeated U.S. 2–1 at Philadelphia, Pa.
1965	Australia defeated U.S. 2–1 at Melbourne, Australia
1966	U.S. defeated W. Germany 3–0 at Turin, Italy
1967	U.S. defeated Great Britain 2–0 at West Berlin, W. Germany
1968	Australia defeated Netherlands 3–0 at Paris, France
1969	U.S. defeated Australia 2–1 at Athens, Greece
1970	Australia defeated W. Germany 3–0 at Freiburg, W. Germany
1971	Australia defeated Great Britain 3–0 at Perth, Australia
1972	South Africa defeated Great Britain 2–1 at Johannesburg, S. Africa
1973	Australia defeated Japan 2–1 at Hamburg, W. Germany
1974	Australia defeated U.S. 2–1 at Naples, Italy
1975	Czechoslovakia defeated Australia 3–0 at Provence, France
1976	U.S. defeated Australia 2–1 at Philadelphia, Pa.
1977	U.S. defeated Australia 2–1 at Eastbourne, England
1978	U.S. defeated Australia 2–1 at Melbourne, Australia

Longest Singles and Doubles

The longest singles match in women's tennis history occurred in 1966 at Piping Rock, Locust Valley, New York, when it took 62 games for Kathy Blake of the U.S. to defeat Elena Subirats of Mexico, 12-10, 6-8, 14-12.

The longest doubles match was the 1964 meeting between Nancy Richey—Carole Graebner and Justina Bricka—Carol Hanks, all of the U.S. Richey—Graebner took 81 games in all, 31-33, 6-1, 6-4, to win this match at South Orange, New Jersey.

Highest Earnings

Christine Evert Lloyd (U.S., born December 21, 1954) earned a record $454,486 in 1978. She has won over 60 per cent of all the tournaments she has entered in her career, including two wins at Wimbledon, two at the French Open, and a record-tying four wins at the U.S. Open (the other four-time national women's champions are Helen Jacobs and Molla Mallory). Only 13 women have ever beaten her, and 5 of them only managed it once, as of the end of the 1978 season.

Virginia Slims

A major step forward in women's professional tennis took place in September, 1970, when eight women professionals who were dissatisfied with the inequitable prize money offered for winners of women's tournaments, set up their own tournament in Houston, Texas. With the assistance of Gladys Heldman, then the editor of *World Tennis Magazine*, and the sponsorship of the Philip Morris Corporation, these eight women—Billie Jean King, Rosemary Casals, Judy Dalton, Peaches Bartkowicz, Val Ziegenfuss, Kerry Melville, Kristy Pigeon and Nancy Richey—took part in the First Virginia Slims Tournament on September 27, 1970, competing for $7,500 in prize money.

The tournament grew quickly in popularity with both players and the public, until in 1978 there were 12 tournaments on a circuit schedule, culminating in the $150,000 Virginia Slims Championship, held in Oakland, California, March 29–April 2, 1978, where Martina Navratilova defeated Evonne Goolagong in the finals to walk off with the $50,000 first prize. The annual championships were held 1972–78, and the winners were as follows:

1972	Chris Evert	1976	Evonne Goolagong
1973	Chris Evert	1977	Chris Evert
1974	Evonne Goolagong	1978	Martina Navratilova
1975	Chris Evert		

In 1978 the Women's Tennis Association decided to dispense with the sponsorship of Virginia Slims, and instead has joined with the Avon Products corporation in setting up a circuit with 11 regular season events and a total purse package of $2.2 million in 1979.

Track and Field

Wyomia Tyus, seen here winning the 100 meter event in the 1968 Olympic in world record time, is reputedly the fastest woman on record.

Track and field athletics date from the ancient Olympic Games. The earliest accurately known Olympiad dates from July, 776 B.C., at which celebration Coroibos won the foot race. As early as the 6th century B.C., Greek women (who were barred from participating in Olympic events) took part in their own contests, known as the Heraean Games. Held every four years, the Games consisted primarily of foot races over a course of approximately 165 yards.

Fastest Runner

The fastest woman's speed is attributed to Wyomia Tyus (U.S., born August 29, 1945), who was reputed to have reached a speed of over 23 m.p.h. in Kiev, U.S.S.R., on July 31, 1965.

First "Even Time" 100 Yards

The first woman to run an "even time" 100 yards was Chi Cheng (later Mrs. Reel) (born March 15, 1944) of Taiwan, when she clocked 10.0 seconds at Portland, Oregon, on June 13, 1970.

Highest Jumper

The greatest height cleared by a woman above her own head is $10\frac{1}{4}$ inches by Tamami Yagi of Japan, who stands 5 feet $4\frac{1}{2}$ inches tall and jumped 6 feet $2\frac{3}{4}$ inches at Matsumoto, Japan on October 19, 1978.

First 5- and 6-Foot Jumps

The first woman to jump 5 feet was Phyllis Green of Great Britain at London on July 11, 1925. The first to clear 6 feet was Iolanda Balas of Rumania (born December 12, 1936), at Bucharest on October 18, 1958.

In the year 1970, when Chi Cheng ran the first 10-second 100 yards ever by a woman, she won all 63 races she entered, setting five world records in the process.

Ulrike Meyfarth (left) became the youngest woman to break an individual world record with a medal-winning high jump at the 1972 Olympics. Dana Zatopkova (right) broke the women's world javelin record when she was 35 years 255 days old.

Youngest and Oldest World Record Breakers

The records for the youngest athletes to break standard world track and field records are both held by women. Ulrike Meyfarth (W. Germany, born May 4, 1956) equalled the world record for the women's high jump at 6 feet 3½ inches, winning the gold medal at the 1972 Munich Olympics, when she was only 16 years 4 months old. Barbara Jones (U.S., born March 26, 1937) was a member of the team which won a gold medal and set a world record in the 4 × 100 meter relay at the 1952 Olympics at Helsinki, Finland, on July 27, at the age of 15 years 123 days.

The oldest woman to break a world track and field record was Dana Zatopkova (*née* Ingrova) (Czechoslovakia, born September 19, 1922), who was 35 years 255 days old when she broke the women's javelin record with a throw of 182 feet 10 inches at Prague, Czechoslovakia, on June 1, 1958.

Women's World and U.S. Track and Field Records

The world records in the following listings are those accepted by the International Athletic Federation as of August 16, 1978. Those marked with an asterisk are awaiting ratification.

As of July 27, 1976, the I.A.A.F. eliminated all records for races measured in yards, except for the mile (for sentimental reasons). All distances up to and including 400 meters must be electrically timed to be considered as records. When a time is given to one-hundredth of a second, it represents the official electrically-timed record.

The U.S. records listed below are those accepted by the Amateur Athletic Union as women's American outdoor records as of November 1, 1978.

Running

Event	min:sec	
100 meters		
World	10.88*	Marlies Oelsner (E. Germany) at Dresden, E. Germany, July 1, 1977
U.S.	11.07	Wyomia Tyus (U.S.) at Mexico City, Mexico, October 15, 1968
200 meters		
World	22.06*	Maritta Koch (E. Germany) at Erfurt, E. Germany, May 28, 1978
U.S.	22.60	Brenda Morehead (Tenn. State U.) at Westwood, California, June 10, 1978
400 meters		
World	48.94*	Maritta Koch (E. Germany) at Prague, Czech., August 31, 1978
U.S.	50.62	Rosalyn Brant (U.S.) at Montreal, Canada, July 28, 1976
800 meters		
World	1:54.9	Tatyana Kazankina (U.S.S.R.) at Montreal, Canada, July 26, 1976
U.S.	1:57.9	Madeline Manning Jackson (U.S.) at College Park, Maryland, August 7, 1976
1,500 meters		
World	3:56.0	Tatyana Kazankina (U.S.S.R.) at Podolsk, U.S.S.R., June 28, 1976
U.S.	4:02.6	Jan Merrill (U.S.) at Montreal, Canada, July 29, 1976
1 mile		
World	4:23.8	Natalia Maracescu (née Andrei) (Rumania) at Bucharest, Rumania, May 22, 1977
U.S.	4:28.2	Francie Larrieu (U.S.) at Mainz, W. Germany, June 28, 1977

Lyudmila Bragina, holder of the women's world record at 3,000 meters, also holds the Olympic record at 1,500 meters for her 1972 performance.

3,000 meters
World	8:27.2*	Lyudmila Bragina (U.S.S.R.) at College Park, Maryland, August 7, 1976
U.S.	8:42.6	Jan Merrill (U.S.) at Oslo, Norway, June 27, 1978

5,000 meters
U.S.	15:35.5	Kathy Mills (Penn State) at Knoxville, Tennessee, May 26, 1978

10,000 meters
U.S.	33:15.1	Peg Neppell (Iowa State T.C.) at Westwood, California, June 9, 1977

The following distances are not on the I.A.A.F. record schedule, and so there are no official world records. However, the performances listed are generally accepted as the best on record for these events.

Event	min:sec	
1,000 meters		
World	2:30.6	Tatyana Providokhina (U.S.S.R.) at Podolsk, U.S.S.R., August 20, 1978
5,000 meters		
World	15:08.8	Loa Olafsson (Denmark) at Copenhagen, Denmark, May 31, 1978

10,000 meters

	31:45.4	Loa Olafsson (Denmark) at Copenhagen, Denmark, April 6, 1978

Marathon

World	2 hr 32:30.0	Grete Waitz (Norway) at New York City, October 22, 1978
U.S.	2 hr 36:24.0	Julie Brown (U.S.) at Eugene, Oregon, September 9, 1978

Hurdles

Event	min:sec	
100 meters		
World	12.48*	Grazyna Rabstzyn (Poland) at Fürth, W. Germany, June 10, 1978
U.S.	13.13	Deby LaPlante (U.S. National Team) at Berkeley, California, July 7, 1978
400 meters		
World	54.89*	Tatyana Zelentsova (U.S.S.R.) at Prague, Czech., September 2, 1978
U.S.	56.61	Mary Ayers (Prairie View T.C.) at Westwood, California, June 11, 1977

Field Events

Event	ft	in	
High Jump			
World	6	7	Sara Simeoni (Italy) at Brescia, Italy, August 4, 1978
U.S.	6	3	Louise Ritter (Texas Women's U.) at College Station, Texas, April 29, 1978
Long Jump			
World	23	3¼	Vilma Bardauskiene (U.S.S.R.) at Prague, Czech., August 29, 1978
U.S.	22	7½	Jodi Anderson (Naturite T.C.) at Westwood, California, June 10, 1978
Shot Put			
World	73	2¾†	Helena Fibingerova (Czech.) at Nitra, Czech., August 20, 1977
U.S.	62	3¼	Maren Seidler (San Jose Stars) at Freising, West Germany, September 10, 1978
Discus Throw			
World	232	0	Evelyn Jahl (*née* Schlaak) at Dresden, E. Germany, August 12, 1978
U.S.	187	2	Lynne Winbigler at Westwood, California, June 10, 1977

---

† Fibingerova set an indoor record of 73 feet 10 inches at Jablonec, Czechoslovakia on February 19, 1977

Kathy Schmidt is the only American holding a current women's track and field world record, for her 1977 javelin throw.

Javelin Throw
World	227	5	Kathryn Joan Schmidt (U.S.) at Fürth, Germany, September 11, 1977
U.S.			same as above

Relays

Event	min:sec	
4 × 100 meters		
World	42.27*	East Germany (Johanna Klier, Monika Hamann, Carla Bodendorf, Marlies Oelsner) at Potsdam, E. Germany, August 19, 1978
U.S.	42.87	U.S. National Team (Barbara Ferrell, Margaret Bailes, Mildred Netter, Wyomia Tyus) at Mexico City, Mexico, October 20, 1968
4 × 200 meters		
World	1:31.6	British Team (Verona Elder, Donna Hartley, Sharon Colyear, Sonia Lannaman) at Crystal Palace, England, August 20, 1977

| U.S. | 1:33.3 | U.S. National Team (Evelyn Ashford, Brenda Morehead, Chandra Cheeseborough, Sandra Howard) at Bourges, France, June 19, 1977 |

4 × 400 meters

| World | 3:19.2 | East German National Team (Doris Maletzski, Brigette Rohde, Ellen Streidt, Christina Brehmer) at Montreal, Canada, July 31, 1976 |
| U.S. | 3:22.8 | U.S. National Team (Debra Sapenter, Sheila Ingram, Pam Jiles, Rosalyn Bryant) at Montreal, Canada, July 31, 1976 |

Mile relay (4 × 440 yards)

| U.S. | 3:30.9 | U.S. National Team (Robin Campbell, Cheryl Toussaint, Madeline Manning Jackson, Debra Sapenter) at Durham, North Carolina, July 19, 1975 |

4 × 800 meters

| World | 7:52.3 | U.S.S.R. National Team (Tatyana Providokhina, Valentina Gerasimova, Svetlana Styrkina, Tatyana Kazankina) at Podolsk, U.S.S.R., August 10, 1976 |
| U.S. | 8:21.2 | U.S. National Team (Julie Brown, Sue Latter, Johanna Foreman, Wendy Knudson) at Bourges, France, June 19, 1977 |

Pentathlon

| World | 4,839 points | Nadezda Tkachenko (U.S.S.R.) at Lille, France, September 19, 1977 (100 meter hurdles, 13.49 sec; shot, 52 ft 3¼ in; high jump, 5 ft 10¾ in; long jump, 21 ft 3½ in; 800 meters, 2 min 10.62 sec) |
| U.S. | 4,704 points | Jane Frederick (L.A. Naturite T.C.) at Nymburk, Czech., June 24–25, 1978 (100 meter hurdles, 13.48 sec; shot, 51 ft 7 in; high jump, 6 ft; long jump, 20 ft 7½ in; 800 meters, 2 min 18.6 sec) |

Most Olympic Medals

The greatest number of Olympic gold medals won in women's track and field is four, achieved by two women. Francina E. Blankers-Koen (Netherlands, born April 26, 1918) won

Fanny Blankers-Koen was 30 years old, with two children, when she won four Olympic gold medals in 1948.

the 100 and 200 meters, 80 meter hurdles and 4 × 100 meter relay, all in 1948. Betty Cuthbert (Australia, born April 20, 1938) won the 100 and 200 meters and the 4 × 100 meter relay in 1956, and the 400 meters in 1964.

The greatest total number of Olympic track and field medals officially won by a woman is seven, a mark equalled by two women, but an interesting finding by researchers gives the record to Shirley de la Hunty (*née* Strickland) (Australia, born July 18, 1925). She won three gold, one silver and three bronze medals in the 1948, 1952 and 1956 Games. However, a recently discovered photo-finish indicates that she finished third, not fourth, in the 200 meters event at the 1948 Games, thus unofficially increasing her medal haul to eight.

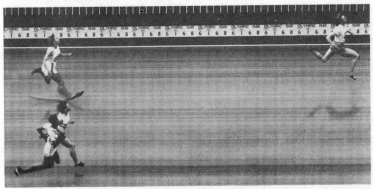

This photo-finish in the 1948 Olympics 200 meter race indicates that Shirley Strickland came in third, not fourth as originally recorded.

Irena Szewinska is shown here winning the 400 meter race at the 1976 Olympics in world record time.

The other athlete with seven officially awarded medals is Irena Szewinska (*née* Kirszenstein) (Poland, born May 24, 1946), who won three gold, two silver and two bronze medals in 1964, 1968, 1972 and 1976. She is the only woman athlete to win a medal in four successive Games.

OLYMPIC GOLD MEDALISTS

100 Meters

1928	Elizabeth Robinson, U.S.	1960	Wilma G. Rudolph, U.S.
1932	Stanislawa Walasiewicz, Poland	1964	Wyomia Tyus, U.S.
		1968	Wyomia Tyus, U.S.
1936	Helen H. Stephens, U.S.	1972	Renate Stecher, E. Germany
1948	Francina E. Blankers-Koen, Neth.	1976	Annegret Richter, W. Germany
1952	Marjorie Jackson, Australia		
1956	Betty Cuthbert, Australia		

Olympic Record: 11.01 seconds by Annegret Richter in a preliminary heat, 1976.

Wilma Rudolph (far right) won the 200 meter race at the 1960 Olympic Games.

200 Meters

1948	Francina E. Blankers-Koen, Neth.	1964	Edith Maguire, U.S.
		1968	Irena Szewinska, Poland
1952	Marjorie Jackson, Australia	1972	Renate Stecher, E. Germany
1956	Betty Cuthbert, Australia		
1960	Wilma G. Rudolph, U.S.	1976	Barbel Eckert, E. Germany

Olympic Record: 22.37 seconds by Barbel Eckert, 1976.

400 Meters

1964	Betty Cuthbert, Australia	1972	Monika Zehrt, E. Germany
1968	Colette Besson, France	1976	Irena Szewinska, Poland

Olympic Record: 49.29 seconds by Irena Szewinska, 1976.

800 Meters

1928	Lina Radke, Germany	1968	Madeline Manning, U.S.
1932–56	Event not held	1972	Hildegard Falck, W. Germany
1960	Ludmila I. Shevtsova, U.S.S.R.		
1964	Ann E. Packer, G.B.	1976	Tatyana Kazankina, U.S.S.R.

Olympic Record: 1 minute 54.9 seconds by Tatyana Kazankina, 1976.

Two gold medals at the 1976 Games went to Tatyana Kazankina, at 800 meters (shown here) and 1,500 meters.

1,500 Meters

1972   Lyudmila Bragina, U.S.S.R.   1976   Tatyana Kazankina,
                                                 U.S.S.R.

Olympic Record: 4 minutes 1.4 seconds by Lyudmila Bragina, 1972.

4 x 100 Meter Relay

1928	Canada	1960	U.S.
1932	U.S.	1964	Poland
1936	U.S.	1968	U.S.
1948	Netherlands	1972	W. Germany
1952	U.S.	1976	E. Germany

Olympic Record: 42.55 seconds by the East German team (Marlies Oelsner, Renate Stecher, Carla Bodendorf, Barbel Eckert), 1976.

4 x 400 Meter Relay

1972   E. Germany   1976   E. Germany

Olympic Record: 3 minutes 19.2 seconds by East German team (Doris Maletzki, Brigitte Rohde, Ellen Streidt, Christina Brehmer), 1976.

Annelie Ehrhardt sails over a hurdle on her way to a 1972 gold medal.

100 Meter Hurdles

1972 Annelie Ehrhardt,
      E. Germany

1976 Johanna Schaller,
      E. Germany

Olympic Record: 12.59 seconds by Annelie Ehrhardt, 1972.

High Jump

1928	Ethel Catherwood, Canada	
1932	Jean M. Shiley, U.S.	
1936	Ibolya Csak, Hungary	
1948	Alice Coachman, U.S.	
1952	Esther C. Brand, South Africa	
1956	Mildred McDaniel, U.S.	
1960	Iolanda Balas, Rumania	
1964	Iolanda Balas, Rumania	
1968	Miloslava Rezkova, Czech.	
1972	Ulrike Meyfarth, W. Germany	
1976	Rosemarie Ackermann, E. Germany	

Olympic Record: 6 feet 4 inches by Rosemarie Ackermann, 1976.

Using her "old-fashioned" straddle style jump, Rosi Ackerman took the high jump gold at the 1976 Games.

Long Jump

1948	V. Olga Gyarmati, Hungary		1964	Mary D. Rand, G.B.
1952	Yvette W. Williams, New Zealand		1968	Viorica Viscopoleanu, Rumania
1956	Elzbieta Krzesinska, Poland		1972	Heidemarie Rosendahl, W. Germany
1960	Vyera Krepkina, U.S.S.R.		1976	Angela Voigt, E. Germany

Olympic Record: 22 feet 5 inches set in Pentathlon competition by Heidemarie Rosendahl, 1972.

Shot Put

1948	Micheline O. M. Ostermeyer, France		1964	Tamara N. Press, U.S.S.R.
1952	Galkna I. Zybina, U.S.S.R.		1968	Margitta Gummel, E. Germany
1956	Tamara Tyshkyevich, U.S.S.R.		1972	Nadyezhda Chizhova, U.S.S.R.
1960	Tamara N. Press, U.S.S.R.		1976	Ivanka Khristova, Bulgaria

Olympic Record: 69 feet $5\frac{1}{4}$ inches by Ivanka Khristova, 1976.

Tamara Tyshkyevich, the 244-pound Russian shot put specialist, won the gold medal in her event in 1956.

Discus Throw

1928	Helena Konopacka, Poland	1956	Olga Fikotova, Czech.
1932	Lillian Copeland, U.S.	1960	Nina Ponomaryeva, U.S.S.R.
1936	Gisela Mauermayer, Germany	1964	Tamara N. Press, U.S.S.R.
1948	Micheline O. M. Ostermeyer, France	1968	Lia Manoliu, Rumania
1952	Nina Romashkova, U.S.S.R.	1972	Faina Melnik, U.S.S.R.
		1976	Evelin Schlaak, E. Germany

Olympic Record: 226 feet 4 inches by Evelin Schlaak, 1976.

Javelin Throw

1932	Mildred Didrikson, U.S.	1964	Mihaela Penes, Rumania
1936	Tilly Fleischer, Germany	1968	Angela Nemeth, Hungary
1948	Herma Bauma, Austria	1972	Ruth Fuchs, E. Germany
1952	Dana Zatopkova, Czech.	1976	Ruth Fuchs, E. Germany
1956	Inese Jaunzeme, U.S.S.R.		
1960	Elvira A. Ozolina, U.S.S.R.		

Olympic Record: 216 feet 4 inches by Ruth Fuchs, 1976.

Pentathlon

1964	Irina R. Press, U.S.S.R.	1972	Mary E. Peters, G.B.
1968	Ingrid Becker, W. Germany	1976	Sigrun Siegl, E. Germany

Olympic Record: 4,801 points by Mary E. Peters, 1972.
Note: Pentathlon has consisted of 100 meter hurdles, shot put, high jump, long jump and 200 meter race. The 200 meter segment has been replaced with an 800 meter race, and this change will be included in the 1980 Olympic event.

Trampolining

The sport of trampolining (from the Spanish word *trampolin,* a springboard) dates from 1936, when the prototype "T" model trampoline was developed by George Nissen (U.S.). Trampolines were used in show business at least as early as "The Walloons," of the period 1910–12. World championships were instituted in 1964.

World Championships—Individual

1964 Judy Wills, U.S.	1972 Alexandra Nicholson, U.S.
1965 Judy Wills, U.S.	1974 Alexandra Nicholson, U.S.
1966 Judy Wills, U.S.	1976 Svetlana Levina, U.S.S.R.
1967 Judy Wills, U.S.	1978 Tatyana Anisimova,
1968 Judy Wills, U.S.	U.S.S.R.
1970 Renee Ransom, U.S.	

Judy Wills (left) held the world championship for five consecutive years.

Volleyball

The game was invented as Minnonette in 1895 by William G. Morgan at the Y.M.C.A. gymnasium at Holyoke, Massachusetts. The International Volleyball Association was formed in Paris in April, 1947. The primary difference between the men's and women's games is that the net is set at 7 feet $4\frac{1}{2}$ inches for women, and 7 feet $11\frac{1}{2}$ inches for men. Women's world championships were instituted in 1952, and volleyball became an Olympic event for both men and women in 1964.

World Championships

Asterisk indicates Olympic title

1952	U.S.S.R.	1968*	U.S.S.R.
1956	U.S.S.R.	1970	U.S.S.R.
1960	U.S.S.R.	1972*	U.S.S.R.
1962	Japan	1974	Japan
1964*	Japan	1976*	Japan
1966	Japan	1978	Cuba

Most Olympic Medals

The only volleyball player to win four medals is Inna Ryskal of the U.S.S.R. (born June 15, 1944), who won a silver medal in 1964 and 1976 and golds in 1968 and 1972.

Walking

24-Hour Record

The best performance for distance walked in 24 hours by a woman is 109.8 miles by Anne Van De Meer (Netherlands) at Rouen, France, on May 20–21, 1978.

"World Records"

There are no official world records for women's walking events, but the following are generally accepted as the "best on record."

Distance (track)	min:sec	
3,000 meters	13:39.6	Siv Gustafsson, Sweden, at Gothenburg, Sweden, July 29, 1977
5,000 meters	23:17.5	Thorill Gylder, Norway, at Oslo, Norway, August 4, 1978
10,000 meters	48:40.0	Thorill Gylder, Norway, at Softeland, Norway, September 16, 1978

Water Skiing

The origins of water skiing lie in plank gliding or aquaplaning. A 19th-century treatise on sorcerers refers to Eliseo of Tarentum who, in the 14th century, "walks and dances" on the water. The first report of aquaplaning was from the Pacific coast of the U.S. in the early 1900's.

The present-day sport of water skiing was pioneered by Ralph W. Samuelson on Lake Pepin, Minnesota, on two curved pine boards in the summer of 1922, although claims have been made

Maria Carrasco scored 5,570 points in trick competition at Milan, September 1977.

for the birth of the sport on Lake Annecy (Haute Savoie), France, in 1920. The first World Water Ski Organization was formed in Geneva, Switzerland, on July 27, 1946. World championships were instituted for men and women in 1949.

Jumping

The first recorded jump on water skis was by Ralph W. Samuelson, off a greased ramp at Lake Pepin, Minnesota, in 1925. The longest jump recorded by a woman is one of 128 feet by Linda Giddens (U.S.) at Miami, Florida, on August 22, 1976.

Slalom

The women's world record for slalom on a particular pass is 3 buoys on a 39-foot line by Cindy Hutcherson Todd (U.S.) at Groveland, Florida, on July 16, 1977.

Tricks

The women's record point score for tricks is 5,570 points by Maria Victoria Carrasco (Venezuela) at Milan, Italy, on September 3, 1977.

Highest Speed

Donna Patterson Brice (born 1953) set the women's water skiing speed record of 111.0 m.p.h. at Long Beach, California, on August 21, 1977.

Barefoot

The first person to water ski barefoot is reported to be Dick Pope, Jr., at Lake Eloise, Florida, on March 6, 1947. The fastest barefoot speed by a woman is 61.39 m.p.h. by Haidee Jones of Australia.

Women's World Championships

Overall

1949	Willa Worthington, U.S.	1963	Jeanette Brown, U.S.
1950	Willa Worthington McGuire, U.S.	1965	Liz Allan, U.S.
1953	Leah Marie Rawls, U.S.	1967	Jeanette Stewart-Wood, G.B.
1955	Willa Worthington McGuire, U.S.	1969	Liz Allan, U.S.
1957	Marina Doria, Switzerland	1971	Christy Weir, U.S.
1959	Vickie Van Hook, U.S.	1973	Lisa St. John, U.S.
1961	Sylvie Hulsemann, Luxembourg	1975	Liz Allan Shetter, U.S.
		1977	Cindy Todd, U.S.

Slalom

1949	Willa Worthington, U.S.	1963	Jeanette Brown, U.S.
1950	Evie Wolford, U.S.	1965	Barbara Cooper-Clack, U.S.
1953	Evie Wolford, U.S.	1967	Liz Allan, U.S.
1955	Willa Worthington McGuire, U.S.	1969	Liz Allan, U.S.
1957	Marina Doria, Switzerland	1971	Christy Freeman, U.S.
		1973	Sylvie Maurial, France
1959	Vickie Van Hook, U.S.	1975	Liz Allan Shetter, U.S.
1961	Janelle Kirkley, U.S.	1977	Cindy Todd, U.S.

Tricks

1949	Madeleine Boutellier, France	1953	Leah Marie Rawls, U.S.
		1955	Marina Doria, Switzerland
1950	Willa Worthington McGuire, U.S.	1957	Marina Doria, Switzerland
		1959	Piera Castelvetri, Italy

1961	Sylvie Hulsemann, Luxembourg	1973	Maria Victoria Carrasco, Venezuela
1963	Guyonne Dalle, France	1975	Maria Victoria Carrasco, Venezuela
1965	Dany Duflot, France	1977	Maria Victoria Carrasco, Venezuela
1967	Dany Duflot, France		
1969	Liz Allan, U.S.		
1971	Willi Stahle, Netherlands		

Jumping

1949	Willa Worthington, U.S.	1965	Liz Allan, U.S.
1950	Johnette Kirkpatrick, U.S.	1967	Jeanette Stewart-Wood, G.B.
1953	Sandra Swaney, U.S.		
1955	Willa Worthington McGuire, U.S.	1969	Liz Allan, U.S.
1957	Nancie Rideout, U.S.	1971	Christy Weir, U.S.
1959	Nancie Rideout, U.S.	1973	Liz Allan Shetter, U.S.
1961	Renate Hansluvka, Austria	1975	Liz Allan Shetter, U.S.
1963	Renate Hansluvka, Austria	1977	Linda Giddens, U.S.

Weightlifting

Amateur weightlifting is of comparatively modern origin, and the first "world" championship was staged at the Cafe Monico, Piccadilly, London, on March 28, 1891. Prior to that time, weightlifting consisted of professional exhibitions in which some of the advertised poundages were open to doubt. There is currently a booming interest in women's weightlifting, with an increasing number of female participants both in women's competitions and testing their brawn against male lifters.

Greatest Lift

The greatest lift ever by a woman is 3,564 lb. with a hip and harness by Mrs. Josephine Blatt (*née* Schauer) of the U.S. (1869–1923) at the Bijou Theatre, Hoboken, New Jersey on April 15, 1895.

Lifting her 182-pound brother was child's play to Katie Sandwina, a 220-pound performer who reputedly lifted 312½ pounds over her head.

The greatest overhead lift ever made by a woman is 286 lb. in a Continental jerk by Katie Sandwina (*née* Brumbach), of Germany (born January 21, 1884, died as Mrs. Max Heymann in New York City, in 1952) in *c.*1911. She stood 5 feet 11 inches tall, weighed 210 lb., and is reputed to have unofficially lifted 312½ lb. and to have once shouldered a 1,200-lb. cannon taken from the tailboard of a Barnum & Bailey circus wagon.

Power Lifts

It was reported that a hysterical 123-lb. woman, Mrs. Maxwell Rogers, lifted one end of a 3,600-lb. car which, after the collapse of a jack, had fallen on top of her son at Tampa, Florida, on April 24, 1960. She cracked some vertebrae.

The highest two-handed dead lift by a woman in competition is 458 lb. by Jan Suffolk Todd (born May 22, 1952 in the U.S.) at Stephenville Crossing, Newfoundland, Canada, on June 24, 1978. She weighed 196½ lb. Her squat, a record 480 lb., and bench press of 187 lb., made a record three-lift total of 1,125 lb.

According to an interview with her husband, Terry Todd,

High school teacher Jan Todd is considered the strongest woman in the world. Her two-handed dead lift record is 458 pounds.

who himself has held 15 world records in powerlifting, Jan Todd decided to pursue competitive weightlifting as a result of the *Guinness Book of World Records*. She reportedly saw a copy which listed the women's weightlifting record as a 392-lb. lift by Mlle. Jane de Vesley in Paris on October 14, 1926, and remarked "I think I can beat that." One year and four months later she did, lifting 394½ lb.

Yachting

Yachting dates from the £100 (now $200) stake race between King Charles II of England and his brother James, Duke of York, on the Thames River, on September 1, 1661, over 23 miles from Greenwich to Gravesend. The earliest club is the Royal Cork Yacht Club (formerly the Cork Harbour Water Club), established in Ireland in 1720. The word "yacht" is from the Dutch, meaning to hunt or chase.

Around-the-World Voyages

At the age of 41, Krystyna Choynowska-Liskiewicz of Poland became the first woman to sail solo around the world. She set out on March 28, 1976 from Las Palmas in the Canary Islands and sailed westward in her 32-foot fiberglass sloop. She crossed her outward track in the Atlantic on March 26, 1978, having made a number of stops en route.

Naomi James of New Zealand sailed around the world via Cape Horn, setting out on September 9, 1977, and arriving back at her starting point, Dartmouth, England, on June 8, 1978. She stopped only twice, at Capetown, South Africa and the Falkland Islands, and between these stopovers achieved the longest non-stop single-handed passage by a woman, totaling 14,000 miles.

Ocean Crossings

The first woman to sail single-handed across the Atlantic was Anne Davison of Great Britain, who left Plymouth, England on May 18, 1952, and landed in Miami, Florida on August 13, 1953. The longest stretch completed without stopping in her small wooden yacht, *Felicity Ann*, was between the Canary Islands and Dominica, a distance of 3,300 miles.

The only solo crossing of the Pacific by a woman was achieved by Sharon Sites of the U.S., a trip which she has completed twice. Her first transpacific voyage was a 39-day passage from San Pedro to Hawaii in a 25-foot sloop, covering a distance of 2,300 miles. On July 24, 1969, she completed a longer journey, covering the 5,000 miles from Yokohama, Japan to San Diego, California in 74 days.

Racing

The first international women's championships were held at Quiberon, France in May, 1974. Organized under the authority of the French national sailing organization, 80 women from 11 countries took part. Martine Allix of France won in the single-handed dinghy class against 28 other competitors, and Gonnede de Vos of the Netherlands won in the two-man dinghy class (420 class) in a field of 26 boats.

Index